So ~~want~~ a Racehorse?

Then follow the highs and lows
of my personal journey

Philip Woodcock-Jones

The Choir Press

Copyright © 2022 Philip Woodcock-Jones

All rights reserved. No part of this publication may be reproduced or transmitted in any form or by any means, electronic or mechanical including photocopying, recording or any information storage or retrieval system, without prior permission in writing from the publishers.

The right of Philip Woodcock-Jones to be identified as the author of this work has been asserted by him in accordance with the Copyright, Designs and Patents Act 1988

First published in the United Kingdom in 2022 by
The Choir Press

ISBN 978-1-78963-333-7

Contents

Desert Orchid	1
Jodami	7
Brandsby Stripe and Bengal Boy	13
The Fellowship of the Rose Partnership	32
Just My Pal	40
Pinch Me Silver	45
Business Class and Ritsi	51
Snow Alert	60
Fiddler's Flight	66
Sedgefield	77
The Junior Man	92
The British Thoroughbred Retraining Centre	96
Black Market	100
So You Want to Own a Racehorse?	104
Horse Racing	116
Types of Races	116
Classes of Races	119
The Handicapping System	120
The Going	122
Entries and Declarations	123
An Afterthought	126

Dedication

This book is dedicated to all the horses past, present and future who have or will add lustre to our lives.

Desert Orchid

I'm not going to pretend that I grew up dreaming of owning a racehorse and that I had to battle through forty-odd long, hard years before finally realising my childhood ambition. It wasn't like that at all. I wasn't even dreaming of being a jockey and riding the winner of the Grand National or indeed being involved with horses in any way, shape or form. Most of the time I was dreaming instead of opening the bowling or maybe even keeping wicket for Derbyshire – a not totally forlorn hope for a time, as I had some ability at the sport and there was a phase when I was about ten that I thought I might be the next Bobby Charlton – although that really was stupid.

However, as a child I loved all sports and at school would have a go at most things – basketball, tennis, rugby as well as cricket and football. I even tried crown green bowls under the guidance of my father when I was about seventeen or eighteen, but the sport I had most access to watching (on the television, at least) was horse racing. At the time (from the late '50s to the mid-'60s) when I was growing up, it had more TV coverage than any other sport. There was no blanket coverage of football as there is today and, although test matches were shown live on the BBC, they were infrequent, only five a summer usually. But every Saturday and, it seemed, quite frequently on weekdays too, you could listen to Clive Graham and Peter O'Sullivan calling the horses, whilst over on ITV I remember John Rickman. He was the dapper, quite posh chap who always wore a trilby and lifted it to you, the viewer, when

So You Want to Own a Racehorse?

they went over to him for a résumé of the betting. Yes, on ITV they actually recognised the existence of betting in racing (shock, horror) whilst the BBC studiously seemed to ignore it for years. Not that I was especially interested in gambling. I never felt any urge to save up my pocket money and get a bet on one of my favourite horses of the day. I suppose I could have done so via my ten-years-older brother Ralph and there was a betting shop conveniently placed to the top of the road.

No, it was everything else that captivated me about the world of horse racing, and still does. The horses themselves, their names and their form figures and the colours that the jockeys wore (although you had to guess somewhat what they really were in the days of black and white telly) and the whole mystery, ritual and terminology of horse racing. That, I think, is what attracted and fascinated me. What did it mean when the man reading out the betting prices said 10 to 1 bar? What was 'bar'? And then what was a gelding? I don't think I ever asked, which was probably just as well. Also, where was Bogside? And why a cross of Lorraine? Who was Lorraine? Setting all that aside, what I think really glued me to the screen was the presence of favourite, familiar horses. Horses that I had almost fallen in love with and, in a way, hero-worshipped like I hero-worshipped Bobby Charlton. Mandarin, Pas Seul, Frenchman's Cove (oh, the wonderful Frenchman's Cove) – then there was Taxidermist and, later, Mill House and Arkle and others. Many others I dare say I have forgotten. But those old favourites, when they were running, somehow it felt as though they belonged to me. So was that the start of a little dream of ownership even then, all those years ago in front of a black and white TV, watching racing from Kempton or Haydock or Newbury or anywhere?

Well maybe, but I'm not going to get it out of proportion. All I can say is that, as a kid, I had equine sporting heroes as well as human ones. Now I just have equine ones. Back then there are certain performances that still stand out. Performances that thrilled me and stayed in my memory. Mill House of England, for instance, beating Arkle of Ireland in the Hennessy. I was an out-and-out Mill House supporter then, before I had realised just how good Arkle was and how unlucky he had been in that Hennessy Gold Cup. Then the 1966 Grand National, which was won by Anglo, trained by Fred Winter and tipped to win by me at 50 to 1! I had followed him for a couple of years and couldn't understand why he wasn't one of the favourites. I was obviously oblivious of the fact that he had lost all his form during the current season, but he was a favourite of mine anyway and I duly told my mother about him and she, when she discovered he was a Fred Winter-trained horse (he was a favourite trainer of hers), bet on him at the local bookies. I imagine it was a shilling or thereabouts each way maybe that she had wagered but there was excitement unbounded as he galloped home by twenty lengths. I don't know how much she won that day but I never saw any of it as a reward for my expert punditry and all I remember is being warned not to tell my father, who was at work on a Saturday. I guess she wanted to keep the winnings herself to spend as she wanted, which was fair enough I suppose and, also, my father was pretty much anti-gambling for whatever reason, and her sloping off to the bookies on Grand National day would not have gone down too well.

After that, and now moving into my adulthood, there was Red Rum wearing down the gallant Crisp after the last fence in the 1973 National, much to my delight. Everyone seemed sorry for Crisp, a two-miler carrying masses of weight and a top-class horse just getting collared on the line, but I had become a Red Rum fan and supporter on the day thanks to my wife (then my girlfriend) who had picked him out as the winner seeing him in the parade ring on the television. He was, she said, by far the best-looking horse in the race. She knew nothing about form, but he

So You Want to Own a Racehorse?

would win, she announced. She obviously had a fine eye for a horse even then and it was in no little part thanks to her that I got into horse racing ownership some twenty-six years later. It was she, in fact, who got me into horses – real actual flesh and blood horses that is, not just TV hero horses. But I'll come back to all that later.

My racing memories then continued but seemed to be centred around other heroic Grand National performances. Red Rum winning again and then again. Aldaniti in 1981 triumphing against all odds (with the jockey on board who was a cancer survivor). My watching of racing though had become seriously curtailed since my childhood because of those two not inconsiderable items getting in the way – life and work. There are so many boring constraints when you're an adult.

However, there were two important turning points for me, looking back, which were to lead to my eventual foray into racehorse ownership. Number 1 – we (my now wife and I) bought a riding horse, at her suggestion in 1979. She loved horses, had ridden as a child and teenager and I thought she was a real equestrian expert. Number 2 – I discovered and was captivated by a new racing hero in the late 1980s. His name was Desert Orchid.

I heard about him from where I know not but after I did hear about him and his exploits he managed, single-handedly to rekindle my interest in National Hunt racing. As I have said, life and work had intervened in the meantime and, although I had actually been sitting on horses myself and learning to ride and managing to stay on board even over smallish jumps and loving it, following racing had somehow ended up taking something of a back seat.

But now this dashing grey, a front runner who became the favourite for the Champion Hurdle but then took up chasing, came along. His style was simple, and he was brilliant. He attacked every fence with relish whilst, seemingly, barely looking at it, took the lead and just kept on galloping out in front until he'd won. Simple. He and he alone reminded me of just how thrilling and wonderful in every way was the sport of jump racing. He reminded me who the real heroes (that word again) of sport were. Not footballers. Not cricketers. No. Horses – so obvious.

There were so many races I can remember him running and they all gave me a nervous expectation beforehand. I would still put him at number 1, above all jump horses I have ever seen even though, logically, Arkle would have beaten him and every other horse hands down on sheer ability. And Red Rum probably remains the nation's favourite with the wider public. But I rate him nevertheless above all the rest – Kauto Star, Denman, Best Mate, Tiger Roll and so on – because of his attitude and charisma. He was a total star.

His win in the 1988 Whitbread Gold Cup was as breathtaking a performance as you will ever see. He held the lead practically all the way round over three miles and six furlongs and yet he could still win over two miles. The Racing Post Chase of 1990 was rated at the time the best handicap performance ever in a steeplechase and I would say remains so. No horse is even asked to give away the chunks of weight that he was doing these days. Not a horse of his class anyway. Nowadays handicaps wouldn't even be a consideration. And then, in the previous year there was his most famous and momentous performance to win the Cheltenham Gold Cup. Oh my God. I watched it in a betting shop (I forget which one, sorry) in Derby and by the time he had finally seen off the challenges of a horse called Yahoo in the mud, nay liquid soil, of Cheltenham, I felt as exhausted, emotionally anyway, as the horse must have done physically. I would say that I would have had no more than £2 each way on him, by the way, so that wasn't the reason. Without having to look again at the race replay, I can see him now swerving to the left on the run-in to intimidate the poor unfortunate Yahoo, whose moment of glory it could have been, and put him firmly in his place – which was second. A marvellous performance because of the left-handed track, which he hated, and the going, which was against him too, supposedly. But he did it!

It was on the back of that one single race and victory that I thought that if seemingly ordinary folk like Richard Burridge (the owner) and family can have a Gold Cup winner, maybe so could I one day. I was approaching my thirty-ninth birthday but still not earning quite enough on a regular basis to seriously think about it, but the seed had been well and truly planted on that wet, wet, March afternoon in the Cotswolds. So, thank you Desert Orchid.

Jodami

My enthusiasm for racing had now been reignited. I started going to race meetings – Uttoxeter was very handy being just a few miles down the road and an excellent course for both viewing and atmosphere. There was always a buzz in the stands before each race and much cheering and shouting from the crowd when they swung into the home straight. Had I gone to, say, Leicester first off I might have gained a less favourable impression of what racing was all about, as there the crowd there seems moribund and the atmosphere is only one up on that of a morgue.

I even planned a trip to Cheltenham the following year for Gold Cup day. It was the year (1990) of the famous (or was it infamous for me?) victory of Norton's Coin at 100–1 with Desert Orchid, the hot favourite, the people's favourite and fresh from his great Racing Post Chase win, finishing third. I had gone to laud Dessie and see him crowned champion again but came away disappointed. But what an arena to watch racing in and even in defeat, after the initial hurt had worn off, the backstory of the winner became apparent.

Sirrell Griffiths, a fifty-one-year old dairy farmer from Carmarthenshire, gets up at 4:30 in the morning and milks his cows, then he loads his horse into the box and drives it over 100 miles across to Cheltenham where, a few hours later, he has won the Gold Cup no less, with a horse he has known since it was a foal, had followed during its early point-to-point career, and had later bought and trained along with a couple of others on his farm. In what other sport could that sort of David and Goliath story have happened? Probably only in jump racing – it could never have occurred on the flat, where big money and expensively-bred horses rule absolutely.

Anyway, all these hopes and dreams of success and elation were duly stored in my brain, ready for the time I could actually afford to start thinking about it. By the way, back in the early '90s syndicate ownership was not a big thing and there was still more of the perception that you had to be a very wealthy person to own a racehorse. So, as far as I was concerned, it was still outside my scope at the time. As I mentioned, we did own our own horses at home at this time – since 1979, in fact, when, I remember, I even had to be shown how to put a head collar on a horse. At first we were at three different livery yards, progressing a little more upmarket at each move and, then, in the mid-'80s we managed to buy our own place. Three acres of England. It was in beautiful, rural South Derbyshire and we had grazing, a stable block, which we had erected and, after a couple of years, an all-weather manège on which to work the horses. Dressage had become our 'thing' – quite a contrast to National Hunt racing you might think, but whatever the equestrian sport, everything revolves around the same animal. And I got to know and love horses pretty quickly and respect them as animals, even though I would never rate myself as a particularly expert dressage rider. But I'm so thankful for that first time my wife sat me on our very first horse all those years ago. It was a real turning point in my life.

Dressage was always a bit too precise and, maybe, fiddly for my temperament I think. There were too many things to think about all at the same time. Cricket (my first love as a sport) is instinctive with not much time to think about which shot you may want to play. Dressage is not. Everything had to be learned and thought about – intellectualised, if you like. My wife was good at that. It suited her. But I played my part helping fittening the horses by going on hacks and then being her 'eyes on the ground'. I got to know what I was looking for, what was correct, what was not, and I knew the theory even if I could not practise it very well myself, but horse ownership (of that kind) did provide me with an impetus to go into racing as an owner because I began to be able to imagine what a trainer would be doing with their horses. The same as us really – getting the horse fit, schooling, feeding the right balance of corn and hay, maybe turning them out into a field for a nibble of grass. Horses, I discovered, were still horses, be they warmbloods (like ours at home) or thoroughbreds, or indeed any other breed for that matter.

Somehow owning a racehorse became more tangible because of my own involvement with horses. It's hard to explain but it seemed less of a giant leap and more of an extension almost of my own equestrian life.

The main problem was still finance, as I touched on earlier. I had been in a pretty well-paid job but (for reasons I won't bore you with and are quite irrelevant anyway) I made a bad career choice and, consequently, my take-home pay took a bit of a tumble. Not to worry. Liz, my wife, had a good job as a teacher and I was confident I would re-establish myself. And I still had more than enough cash to enjoy my racing as a spectator and our own horses as a rider.

The next turning point, however, came in 1993. It is easy to pinpoint because that was the year that Jodami won the Cheltenham Gold Cup. It was another lovely racing story. A small trainer (although massive by Sirrell Griffiths standards) who had been in the point-to-point world until relatively recently, had this big, magnificent looking, dark bay horse, an old-fashioned chaser who had still been fast enough to win his first bumper (National Hunt flat race), and came down from Yorkshire to slay the might of Lambourn and, indeed, France.

The Fellow, trained by Francois Doumen, was one of the favourites and looked as though he was going to be a very difficult horse to beat. Peter Beaumont was Jodami's trainer and he had been a late starter under National Hunt rules. He was fifty-eight in that March 1993 and had held a full licence for only about seven years. He kept about a couple dozen horses in his yard and it was noticeable, I thought, that when, some years later, he had occasion to give me one of his business cards, he described himself as a 'trainer and farmer'. He was a real old-fashioned (that phrase again) stockman with an eye for a horse, and he had picked an outstanding one in Jodami.

I really can't remember if I had had any money on him for the Gold Cup. I may have had my customary £2 each way, but what I do know is that I really wanted him to win. And seeing him come over the last, take up the running and ease away was a thrilling feeling. What must it feel like if it was your own horse? Your horse, who you had seen come over from Ireland just backed, start his training, go through bumpers into novice hurdles and then, eventually, start steeplechasing. It would be indescribable. The thing was, too, that he was my (and my wife's) type of horse. Wide-chested, plenty of bone and substance. The sort that filled your eye. The sort to take you on a day's hunting across Leicestershire even. The fact that he stayed the three miles two furlongs would be no surprise but to have the speed to win a Gold Cup was truly amazing. Anyway, in March 1993 he became my new favourite and another equine hero even if by now I was in my forties.

Now, as it happened – and this was sheer chance – we had booked a few days holiday in North Yorkshire in the April of that year. It was at a farmhouse on the edge of the North York Moors that did bed, breakfast and a superb evening meal. The proprietors even became friends of ours over the years because we became 'regulars'. We visited once, maybe twice a year for a few days at a time.

Jodami

The day we met Jodami we were having a drive around the district and admiring the views when we happened upon the village of Brandsby. As soon as I saw the sign I said to Liz that I thought this was the village where Peter Beaumont trained his lovely big, black horse. I wondered if we could find his farm and maybe he might just let us have a glimpse, just the merest glimpse of his famous gelding. Luckily there was an old red telephone box near to the post office in the centre of the village and, inside, was also a local telephone directory. All this sounds very old-fashioned I'm sure, but there were no smart phones then, as amazing as that may sound to people under a certain age. I looked up his number, phoned and got through. I then launched into a eulogy about his horse and how much we admired him and how great a racing fan I was and so on and so on. And if only we could have even the shortest of looks at Jodami we would be eternally grateful, if we weren't getting in his way that is, and it was convenient to him, otherwise... 'Aye,' Peter interrupted, 'give me twenty minutes. I'm just finishing me dinner. I'll tell you how to get here from the phone box.'

I had no idea what sort of reception I might get but his friendliness shone through immediately even down the telephone line. I could also detect straight away how proud he was of his horse. We duly found his premises, Foulrice Farm, and were warmly greeted there by Peter. Then Jodami (who had been turned away after his victory) was got in from the field by Peter's daughter Anthea who, of course, had been the first woman to ride a winner over the Grand National fences a year or two earlier. The horse was proudly paraded up and down for us for a while then allowed to have a pick of grass in front of the stable block and we were very grateful and thought that that would be that. We already thought they had gone out of their way for us, but no! I think it was about two hours later when we finally took our leave after we had had a full directed tour of the yard by Peter. He introduced us to all his twenty-plus horses that he had in training, plus his young stock, plus one that he tried to sell us as a potential dressage horse. It was too slow to be a racehorse. It seemed as much a pleasure to him to show off his horses as it was for us to see them all.

As we eventually walked back to our car to resume what was left of our afternoon, I turned to Liz and said, 'Well, I tell you, if ever one day I do have enough money to have a racehorse, this is the place I'd want it to be.'

It was quite an epiphany and I think the moment I decided I was damn well going to earn enough to have a racehorse or, at least, a share in one. I knew from that day onwards that I wanted to get involved in the world of racing and training.

Brandsby Stripe and Bengal Boy

Fast forward about six years to 1999 and we're back again at Foulrice Farm, Brandsby, to drop in on Peter again. We were having another long weekend break and I had phoned him the day before to arrange a visit. We were wise to the fact this time that we would probably have another directed tour of the stables and be there all afternoon, but I did have another motive. This time I wanted to sound him out about ownership via a syndicate, partnership or whatever you want to call it. I now had a good, progressive, settled job and I was pretty sure I had the means to do it at last.

Now, in the intervening years I had bumped into Peter at least a couple of times at meetings at Uttoxeter, my local track. I can certainly recall congratulating him profusely on the occasion of Young Kenny's victory in a Midlands Grand National earlier that year. He was one of his new stars following the retirement of Jodami. Kenny had just a run a wonderful race under Brendan Powell and had landed a significant prize, and after I had enthused to Peter about it he just said in his understated way, 'Aye, that was quite good wasn't it?' You could say that again!

However, back to our Foulrice Farm visit. I think we did have another full tour and I know I did discover that Young Kenny didn't have a sweet tooth – he turned his nose up at a Polo as if I was trying to poison him. Most importantly though, Peter gave me a couple of names and contact numbers for two people running partnerships in his yard. In those days partnerships could only have up to twenty members, syndicates could have up to 100. I remember that one of the partnerships was run by a fellow in North East England and that it turned out no good for me. They had a nice horse who had already won one race but the initial outlay was too much for me and they were only selling 10 per cent shares, I think. That meant that the monthly outlay would have been just beyond my range at the time.

The second partnership was run by a person called Paul Clarkson, who lived somewhere in Lancashire and they had just acquired an unraced, homebred store horse from Peter who was by Nomadic Way and unnamed as yet. I guessed that this might be the one for me.

For some reason that I really can't recall now, it took me a month or maybe two to pluck up courage to phone Paul Clarkson. It seemed a very big and important step for me to take and yet I knew I definitely wanted to do it. I did eventually phone, of course, and he told me all about the horse and the cost. £400 would be towards the purchase and I think he said people usually paid about £40 per month for his keep. He was slightly vague about the actual monthly cost but I remember thinking that it seemed all well within my budget and that, finally, I could do it!

I remember phoning Paul back to say that, in principle, I was more than happy to buy a share in a racehorse with him and pay my monthly subscription, but I guess I still wanted a few more details about the whole procedure before I went ahead with it. It seems very cautious now but I was taking a giant leap!

He said, 'Look, I'm at Sedgefield racecourse next week. I'm

doing a presentation in one of the boxes before racing, giving tips for the day, that sort of thing, and then I'm booked in to do the racecourse presenting afterwards. I know it's a bit of a trek for you but if you can make it I could see you there and talk you through everything you need to know and you could make your decision. You'd also be able to meet some people from my other partnership that I've got with Peter. They have a runner there that day.'

Now it is true that Sedgefield is nearly 150 miles away from where I live but, by sheer chance, I was going to the North East that very day and the day after to train a new recruit for my sales team. I was sales manager for an educational supply firm by now. I very quickly worked out that, with an early start and timing everything to perfection, I should be able to meet Paul at Sedgefield racecourse on that afternoon and have a chat. It was September and, therefore, racing didn't start until later and he was tied up first thing anyway with his hospitality box. It was a piece of luck and took some manoeuvring of my timetable, but it could be done – and was.

On the day, we had our chat as planned and he went over the costs again, none of which seemed too frightening or off-putting, and it was all agreed that I should join the Brandsby Racing Partnership, as it was known, with a 5 per cent share as soon as I got the money to him. Then he said, 'I've just spotted some of the connections of the horse we've got running here today. I'll introduce you to them and they can have a word with you. They'll be more than happy to do so.' The horse, he said, was called, rather grotesquely, I thought, 'Top of the North Racing'. Yes, that was the actual name of the horse. Whoever thought to name a horse that? But I was duly introduced to a person called Jean. She was probably in her late sixties I should guess, and very friendly and welcoming and just speaking to her I knew I had made the right decision. Immediately she said, 'Oh, come and see our horse when she comes down into the saddling box and you can come into the parade ring with us as well, if you want.' I wondered if that would be a problem – after all I wasn't an owner of any horse yet and certainly not theirs. I was just there to find out about it all. But, 'No, it'll be all okay. Just follow me.'

So twenty minutes or so before the start of her race I went down with Jean to the saddling boxes 'You'll be able to meet Penny. We've had so much fun with her. Did you see that she won that super seller here last year? It was great. It was like our Gold Cup. I was on a high for the rest of that night and all the way driving back home to Mansfield.' All I could think to say was 'Penny? Who's Penny?' 'Oh it's what we call her. It's her stable name.' Ah, very wise, I thought with an awful racing name like that.

Suddenly I realised I was already achieving some of my racing ambitions. Here I was walking down with an owner to the saddling boxes and the pre-parade ring (sacred ground up until then) to see a real racehorse being saddled up to do battle. And minutes later – there she was – Penny. A brightish bay mare who looked more like a chaser than a hurdler even though it was a hurdle race she was about to run in. There was a group of several people, all from the syndicate of about twenty people that owned her, and I was introduced to some of them as someone who had come along because he was wanting to become an owner with Peter. That sounded very good. I remember following the horse with the others into the parade ring and shaking hands with Peter at some point. We had of course, already met. I also remember looking around as jockeys made their way across the grass to their respective little knot of owners and thinking, 'My God, I'm already standing in the middle of a parade ring like a real owner, shaking hands and talking to trainers and jockeys.' I had never imagined I would doing all this at the start of the day. It actually got a bit better that day too because Penny, who I don't think was among the favourites for the race even though she did have some decent form, ran excellently and finished second. I was invited, therefore, to go into the winner's enclosure to greet her on her return, but I think I declined that honour, feeling that it would be, perhaps, a little fraudulent to get in on the celebrations. By then I was happy enough and thought, 'What a wonderful afternoon – my best racing experience so far and that was as an outsider, so to speak. On the fringes.' If I ever had any lingering doubts I now had none and so the next day I contacted Paul Clarkson and told him my £400 cheque for the purchase of my share (5 per cent) of the horse was on its way and that the standing order for my monthly subscription was set up. Looking back, that was a highly significant day in my life. A day that did change my life and for the better, I hastened to add, forever.

But what was the horse I had just purchased my share in? What did it look like? Was it going to be any good? Had it even got four legs? I had, in fact, taken everything on trust. I was told by Paul that the intention was to have a four-year-old unraced bay gelding that had been home bred by Peter Beaumont. It was out of his brood mare 'I'm Fine' and was by Nomadic Way who, of course, was famous as a Stayers Hurdle winner at the Cheltenham Festival and had also been twice runner up in the Champion Hurdle. He had also been placed on the flat in both the Cesarewich and the Ascot Gold Cup.

Our horse, when I did go and see him, was a big baby with a white stripe down his face but seemed to be very well put together. Like all of Peter's horses, he looked like a future chaser even at that early stage. He was unnamed and there was to be a sort of competition amongst the syndicate (it was already nearly fully subscribed) to choose a name for him. Everyone could suggest a name and then there would be a vote to see which was the most popular – except you could not vote for your own suggestion. However, first, Paul told me there was to be an owners' open day at Peter's in a week or two on a Sunday morning. We could go up, have a good look at our unnamed horse, see him on the gallops along with most of Peter's other horses and partake in a bacon sandwich or two whilst having a general good look around. So that's just what Liz and I did and that was when I first met the members of our syndicate and was welcomed aboard.

As far as our horse was concerned, I seem to remember, although he looked big and magnificent, he blundered his way over some poles because he couldn't be bothered to have a proper look at them. He was too busy looking round him instead. But we excused him that and I, naïvely, began to dream of Cheltenham. It was early October and, with a bit of luck and if all went to plan, he would be ready to race in a bumper sometime around Christmas. He was a clean slate, decently-bred, trained by a top trainer, looked good – what could possibly go wrong?

It wasn't long before we had a name for him too. He was to be known as Brandsby Stripe. Brandsby from the name of the village he was born and trained in. Stripe because of his big, white stripe on his face. We had regular updated telephone bulletins about him from Paul. You dialled up a number and the message played in those pre-email days and there seemed everything to look forward to. I could hardly wait for his debut, which would be in a bumper, but, as with all trainers, 'ready by Christmas' turned by December into 'sometime in the new year'. Still, not to worry. We had plenty of time on our side.

However, New Year came with the news Stripe had thrown a splint. If that means little to you it meant straight away that he would not be able to do any serious work for several weeks. A splint is a common occurrence in a young horse and is basically a bony enlargement that forms on the immature bones of the leg and causes lameness for a while. There is nothing you can do about it except let it form, at which point the lameness disappears. Ah well, I thought, no racing now, as an owner at least, until the spring. I was already discovering that patience was probably the most essential virtue to have if you were a racehorse owner.

Eventually the splint finished growing and he was back in training and finally deemed fit enough to be entered for his much-awaited debut race. I think, in hindsight, he may have been somewhat 'undercooked' as they say, because Peter was keen to give the group a runner before the end of the season. It was now late March, early April when he was entered for a bumper at Carlisle and the sight of his name in print in the Racing Post was a huge thrill to me. For years I had seen plenty of names of other people's horses in print in that august publication, but now it was my turn, albeit I had but a 5 per cent share of that name.

It was another significant day in my life when I went to Carlisle for his first race. After all, it was my first race too. I remember phoning Paul to reserve my badge and being told that I would have to pay half price as all the quota of free badges had already been taken. But that was quite all right by me. I also recall I had driven back 174 miles from Taunton on a business trip the day before and that it was 174 miles in the other direction to get to Carlisle the following day. Absolutely no problem. I would have driven to Land's End via John O'Groats if needs be. I wasn't going to miss my first opportunity to enter a racecourse as an owner.

His race, being a bumper, was, of course, the last of the day, so there was plenty of waiting around and plenty of anticipation time. And I did bump into several of my co-owners during the course of the afternoon. But the outcome of it all was, almost inevitably, an anti-climax. Stripe went off at a big price. Let's face it, he didn't look like a bumper horse. He was too big for that and a bit babyish too. He was always towards the rear, never got in the race and finished next to last of about sixteen. It sounds like, on the face of it when put it in those cold blooded terms, a huge let-down. However, when I eventually returned home down the M6 later that night and reported back to my wife on the events of the day, I told her how much I had enjoyed the whole experience and that it had been absolutely great and that I wouldn't have missed it for anything in the world. Irrationality and eternal hope are two other required virtues.

Of course, a week later, he had thrown another couple of splints and so that was that for the season. He was to be turned out for the summer, after which his legs would have recovered and he would be got back up ready for a campaign in the autumn. Autumn, I suspected, would probably turn into November/December, so more patience required. It really is no good expecting a horse to be got fit and ready to run in a week or two and then go racing every weekend, especially with National Hunt horses too.

When he was got back in from his field there followed plenty of reports from Paul as to his progress. I made a few visits to Peter's to see Stripe working and later being schooled, since he was now intended to go straight to hurdling. And, eventually, the day of his next race was approaching. I didn't think we ever got as far as knowing where or when it would be exactly but he was going to start off in a two-mile novice hurdle. Then the message left by Paul. It went something like this – 'Well, I'm afraid there is bad news about Stripe. I spoke to Peter earlier today and he told me that, sadly, Stripe has broken down in front. In fact he has broken down on both of his front legs which is very unusual and it does mean he will need a year's rest in order to recover.' What a shattering blow. It was hard to take it in but as soon as I heard the words I could work out that it would be at least 18 months before he would see the racecourse again, if he ever saw one again at all. What now? Did I keep paying for a horse who is going to be turned out in a field for a year? Would he be okay again eventually or wouldn't he? The tribulations of ownership had suddenly hit me full in the face and I had only been to one race so far!

I can't remember the exact timescale but I do know that I spoke to Paul fairly shortly afterwards and that, somewhat to my relief, he indicated that Peter had a horse on offer that would be suitable for us as a replacement on an interim basis. We had enough money in our account to purchase him and, on the big plus side, he was fit and ready to run. In fact he had already run in three bumpers and a novice hurdle in the colours of Trevor Hemmings and had shown a little promise. Not enough promise though for Mr Hemmings, who was later to become a Grand National winning owner and who was rich enough then to own a string of horses stationed at a variety of trainers. The horse's name was Bengal Boy (stable name Benny) and, to be honest, what choice did we have?

So we acquired a new horse. I did phone round some of the other owners in our group and all agreed that this was clearly the best idea and pretty rapidly Benny became our property. And as for poor Stripe, well, he was banished to the field for a year with us all wishing him a successful recovery.

Bengal Boy was about to be given an entry and I remember going up to Peter's to meet our new star not long before he was entered for a race at Perth. That was, sadly, going to be a no-go for me. It's an awfully long way to Perth. I remembered Benny from a year or so earlier when I'd seen him at the open morning and, at that time, he had looked like a complete mad head, ready to disappear down the gallops in a cloud of dust at the slightest chance. But since then he had raced a few times, maybe calmed down a bit and, after all, he had shown that slight hint of promise – fourth in a novice hurdle at Bangor behind a half-decent horse. I consoled myself with that thought and hoped for the best as I prepared to cheer him on from a distance.

I watched the Perth race in a betting shop somewhere in Derby and immediately noticed that there had been some money for him and that his price had shortened quite a bit. There seemed to be a bit of a buzz for him and I heard his name being mentioned by punters in the bookies. Well, it certainly wasn't my money that had done it. I've already mentioned my betting limits. Off they went in this novice hurdle in faraway Perth in what had become pretty bottomless conditions. There were slight butterflies in the stomach at the start but halfway through the race the butterflies increased and increased again as, turning in for home, he seemed to be going as well as anything. He had a definite chance. I could hardly believe it. Then, all of a sudden, disappointment as he seemed to hit a complete hole and weakened very quickly and was promptly pulled up by Russ Garrity. For a second I thought 'Oh no, not another lame horse,' but, on speaking on the phone after the race to Paul, I found I need not have worried. Benny, indeed, had hit that proverbial 'hole' and his tank had emptied. Russ had done the right thing in pulling him up on what was atrocious going. So it had been an in and out, up and down sort of start to Bengal Boy's racing career with us but he did certainly look like a race horse.

The next race was run in much faster conditions at Sedgefield one evening. I had done nearly a full day's work in Cheshire and then drove across and up to County Durham to take in the event. Dennis Grattan rode him this time under instructions to hold him up, instructions which were well and truly ignored by the horse at least (I'm not sure what choice the jockey had). To use the technical term Benny 'pissed off' without much control and had a 20+ length lead on the first circuit. Inevitably, he ran out of gas and was once again pulled up. No one seemed to know why he had gone mad like that that night. He had never done it before and he never did it again. But oh dear. Two races for us and two Ps by his name. In truth, although we always travelled with some hope to his races Benny's novice hurdling career never really took off. We all thought he had some ability but he seemed to struggle to get home in his races. He shaped well in both straight novice races and also in handicaps but then ran out of steam in the home straight. He ended his novice season with the lowly handicap mark of 72, but Peter thought he might be better over fences even though he wasn't an over big horse. Peter also had another idea and that was to give him a soft palate operation. Even though he had never made any gurgling noises he thought it might still be a wind problem that was preventing him getting home. A soft palate operation, by the way, is a very common operation performed on lots of racehorses. A few trainers even have it done on all their horses annually as a preventive measure. It involves the cauterization of two flaps of tissue in the horse's throat that can prevent it from drawing in all the air that it needs when it is galloping flat out. For an ordinary riding horse that wouldn't matter, but racehorses are asked to perform at the extremes. It is not an expensive procedure, doesn't take long for the vet to do and has a pretty quick recovery time.

So the summer came and went and in the autumn it was off to Bangor-on-Dee for Benny's chasing debut. He had schooled well over fences and had been duly operated on. But there was only one way to find out if it had had a beneficial effect – and that was on the racecourse. It was my very first time at Bangor and I can remember being baffled by the fact you couldn't get level with the winning post. You watch the races from a grass bank (no stands) with the horses coming at you head on. Thank goodness that big screens had come in by the turn of the century and you could watch finishes at Bangor in the normal, side-on way via them.

We must have all been travelling hopefully but, I'm afraid, another disaster! Benny clobbered an early fence very hard, couldn't get into any sort of rhythm, then hit another fence and Dennis Grattan pulled him up. What an anti-climax. Nothing had been proved except, perhaps, that he did not look like a natural fence jumper. In fact, at home he did eventually earn the soubriquet 'Benny the birch breaker'. Rather unkind, I thought. Oh well. Another P by his name but it was Doncaster next for him and a new jockey – a conditional by the name of David O'Meara. We had never heard of the lad but Peter thought he was all right. He was, of course, to become better known, some years later, as a very successful trainer, mainly of flat horses. Benny was 50 to 1 in this novice handicap chase which didn't look the strongest one ever held at Doncaster which is a grade one course after all. But there were one or two hot shots, nevertheless, who were expected to have the race to themselves. The first objective was for Benny to complete. He was actually managing to get over the obstacles this time even if he did get a bit low over a few. One of the 'hot shots' conveniently fell, which helped our cause, and coming off the final bend, just at the point he used to find nothing more in his hurdle races, the horse started to make a forward move. He was picking up really well. Really, really well and, all of a sudden, at the final fence he had a live chance. It was between him and one other horse but, at the line, although he was still gaining, he couldn't quite reach the winner. He was beaten into second but only by about one length. We could scarcely believe it. Benny had finally proved he had some ability and might one day go one better. It was a nice each-way bet too, which won us all a little bit of money. His wind op seemed to have made all the difference and the only downside was that the handicapper decided to raise him no less than 25lb in the handicap for finishing second.

We returned to Doncaster with high hopes nevertheless for a similar race several weeks later with his starting price now down into single figures. But, what do you know? He jumped very stickily at the first fence and about three fences later crashed into it, jettisoning David onto the floor. Benny had a good old gallop around Doncaster riderless though. And we had had another disappointment. I think I had already learned that you couldn't take anything for granted with racing or, indeed, horses in general. However, there is always the next race to anticipate, providing the horse is okay and Benny had come through his mishap unscathed.

There were more ups and downs with Benny but eventually his day did come – back at Bangor. Everything seemed to go perfectly for him on that day and he eased past the other horses entering the home straight in pretty heavy going and scored by about twenty lengths. All I know is our collective hearts were in our mouths as he approached the last fence well clear. We knew all he had to do was to step over it to win but we never did trust Benny and his jumping. But he got over it in an okay fashion and I had sampled my first taste of victory as an owner. Nothing like it! Hugs all round, pictures taken, champagne, general euphoria.

Benny never did win for us again, although he threatened to do so several times when he got placed and was desperately unlucky not to have won more than the once. But it was not to be. I certainly remember the near misses. At Perth in a hurdle race when he just couldn't quite get up at the line. Also, notably at Perth again, this time in a chase, and ridden again by David O'Meara. I was unable to get up to Scotland, hardly surprisingly, and chose to go into Burton-upon-Trent to find a bookmakers from which to watch the race. It was an evening meeting, one of their summer meetings, and I stood transfixed as Benny set off, took the lead, ran the rest ragged and was leading by probably about twenty-five lengths at the last. He just had to clear the final obstacle in whatever style he chose to give him his second victory. He was bound to do it – and at quite a good price I seem to remember. I was even mentally planning a phone call home to ask my wife to put a bottle of champagne we had in the fridge for my return. But oh no! David, unaccountably, chose to fire him at the last fence and Benny, as we know never the soundest jumper, hit it hard and unseated the aforementioned jockey. Suddenly – disaster when it could have been glory.

Then, in the very last race, as it turned out, that Benny ran for us, he went to Cartmel and, again, I couldn't make the trip up to the Lake District. Work sometimes got in the way of my racing in those days. So I was back in the bookies again (a different one this time actually) watching and hoping and praying as always. David was back on board again and this time he was hurdling. Peter tended to chop and change him for whatever reason. David fired him off at a great pace in front on this occasion, as he had done in that fateful Perth steeplechase. I wasn't really hopeful of him staying in front for the entire duration of the race, but over the last he was still at the head of affairs and with no apparent serious challenger. Then with a very late spurt came a horse named Romil's Star, I seem to recall, who got up and joined him for the last few strides. They were neck and neck and, to my eye, inseparable. An obvious photo finish and, I thought, with luck he might well have held off his late challenger. In those days photo finishes took a little longer to come through compared to today, especially as this was going to be a very tight decision.

Now, in the betting shop was a local racing sage and pundit who seemed to be there every time I went in that particular establishment. I think he had a permanent reserved seat there. He sidled across to me and asked if I'd had a big bet on one or other of the two horses involved because I seemed very excited and agitated. I explained that Bengal Boy was my (or, at least, our) horse. I was the owner.

'Oh,' he said, 'he ran a good race, but he's not won. He just got necked.'

'Are you sure?' I said 'how can you tell?'

'Oh,' he responded, 'he ran a good race, a very good race, but he didn't win it.'

Cue the announcement of the winner, which confirmed the sage's opinion. The distance was a short head but nowadays it would have been a 'nose' I think. 'Noses' didn't exist then as an official distance. And that was that. Another near miss for Benny.

As I said, that turned out to be his last race for us because Stripe, by that time, had been back running for us as well. We had, effectively, been running two horses for the price of one that season thanks to Benny's prize money. Also, Stripe had won a race for us (more of that shortly). So Paul called a meeting to decide which of the two horses we would keep. We couldn't afford two for another year unless everyone wanted to double their subscriptions, which they clearly didn't. So a meeting of all the partners (about fifteen of us, I think) was convened at a hotel at Scotch Corner. There it was voted that Brandsby Stripe would be the chosen one – I think on the grounds that he may develop more than Benny, who had had his chances. He would, sadly, go to the sales at Doncaster. When Benny did go to the sales, thankfully, he was bought by a lovely, caring lady who wanted him to run in point-to-points for her. She lived in Lincolnshire, was Irish and a former teacher who had married a farmer and wanted to be involved in racing, hands on, in one way or another. The horse went on to win one point-to-point for her at Garthorpe. I'm pleased to say that I, along with a few other former owners, went to see him in his new home and also to see him racing in a couple of his points, although not his winning one. Good old Benny. Not a star but a horse that gave me and others a tremendous amount of pleasure. He had a great attitude to his work and to his races, even if things didn't always work out quite as you would have planned.

That closed the Bengal Boy chapter, but now back to Brandsby Stripe. He had come back into training during the previous summer and was ready to run at the start of the proper season. I don't really count summer jumping as being 'proper' even now. Benny's winnings from the previous season, where he had won once and been placed on a number of occasions, were enough, we decided, as I mentioned, to run two horses without having to raise our monthly subscriptions.

Stripe, being a big horse and, by the way, a super and very secure jumper, was never realistically going to win hurdle races. But, of course, he started off in novice hurdles and got fairly soundly beaten without exactly disgracing himself. He did, however, earn himself a reputation for being a lazy horse and lacking concentration. He liked to have a good look around him at the view, even when in mid-race. He did improve slightly through his hurdles career and in his very last hurdle race he did manage an honourable fourth place and a tiny bit of prize money at Sedgefield. Peter, however, always a through and through chasing man, wanted to get him going over fences as quickly as possible. So he was duly schooled and then entered for his first chase at Bangor-on-Dee. It was 2 May by now and this coincided with the impending end of Benny's season as well.

At that time (the regulations keep on changing) he could go straight into a novice handicap chase off his hurdles rating which was pretty (no very) low. Around 70 I think. We had David O'Meara on board and none of us expected anything too much from Stripe on that wet evening in North Wales. But it proved to be the setting for what turned out to be his greatest achievement.

There was a red-hot favourite in the field who had dominated proceedings, but Stripe was still, surprisingly, in the mix approaching the last. The favourite looked a certain winner but, my God! We might just get a place. Fantastic! Wait though. The last fence. The favourite crashes through it when he only had to step over it. He's down – and look who has been handed the lead. Brandsby Stripe! He was challenged flat out to the line by a horse called Lord Brex, a grey that a few years earlier had been a very smart hurdler (winning the Glenlivet Hurdle at Aintree, I think) but who had since lost his way – hence the lowly company he was now keeping. But all that was irrelevant as Stripe, somehow, managed to keep his head in front at the line. It was another photograph but this time we were confident that we would be on the right side of the judge's decision. And yes – the announcement – first number, whatever he was, Brandsby Stripe. More ecstasy, more champagne. And the joy amongst us was even greater because this victory had come out of nowhere and had been totally unexpected. We had had doubts as to Stripe's ability to be a proper racehorse, but he had proved us doubters wrong. The group of owners who were there were exultant of course, but I can still remember David O'Meara jumping off the horse in the winner's enclosure and saying over and over, 'Oh he's a lazy horse, he's a lazy horse.' David was worn out and had been pushing and shoving him along all the way round. In the replay you could actually see the 'lazy horse' admiring a flock of sheep grazing in the centre course instead of concentrating on his jumping and galloping. At the time it didn't really matter to us at all because we had just won again. I was on a personal 'high' for a day or two, scarcely able to believe he had actually done it. I had to keep checking the result but there it was – first place, Brandsby Stripe.

He did return a couple of weeks later to Bangor for a similar race and went off at a much shorter price, but a repeat performance was not to be. He never really got into the race and, although momentarily it looked as though he might progress a bit, in the end he finished about fifth without ever making a challenge. In fairness, he did look a bit tired and Peter thought he'd probably done enough for the season. So he went out for his six-week summer break on the grass.

It was at this point that the aforementioned meeting at Scotch Corner was called and the decision made about Benny's fate. Generally, it was agreed (although I begged to differ) that, because Stripe was the younger horse and had just won a race, he was the better long-term prospect. So we kept him. However, my fears over him were eventually, sadly, borne out. He never did win for us again. In fact, I cannot remember him gaining another place, although my memory may be faulty on that. He certainly never learned how to concentrate on his work. If he had been a human I think that dear old Stripe would have been quite happy to have been a couch potato. I don't think he ever quite got why he had to do all this galloping and jumping round in a circle. Such unnecessary exertion! At Hexham one day for example, after travelling quite nicely for the first circuit, he got to the start of the second circuit and thought he had done quite enough for one day. He planted his feet like an old mule and refused to budge.

Eventually it was decided to retire him from racing as he did not seem to be exactly cut out for it, mentally at least. Physically he was always a rather magnificent looking specimen. Luckily, one of the owners was able to offer him a great home. Their teenage daughter wanted a horse for show jumping and that is how Stripe ended his days at horse shows in County Durham and being a young girl's best friend.

The only unfortunate thing about this was the way in which he eventually met his end some years later. It was so sad when we learned of it. He was in the collecting ring before a show jumping competition when another horse lashed out and kicked him, instantly breaking his leg. To think that he had survived all that racing only to meet his demise in such a way. Horses can be, ironically, both so tough and yet so fragile.

So, with the slightly premature retirement of Stripe, the Brandsby Racing Partnership, as we were known, led by Paul Clarkson, seemed to be at an end. There were no plans for a new horse and its members drifted away. However, there were friends and acquaintances and contacts I had made and it had given me a fantastic introduction to the world of horse racing as an owner. If anyone were thinking of ownership, however wealthy they may be, I would strongly recommend them joining a partnership (or syndicate, as they are now termed) if only because of the social aspect. You get to know so many like-minded people and can share, as we did, the ups and downs, the elations and the frustrations of horse ownership. Someone else is also dealing with all the paperwork and the bill paying and so on, whilst you can just get on with the excitement and pleasure of going racing.

The Fellowship of the Rose Partnership

Meanwhile, I was suddenly horseless, or racehorseless anyway. We still had our dressage horses at home and we rode practically every day. But I soon must have started suffering withdrawal symptoms from not being able to go into the 'owners and trainers' at race meetings. Just going as an ordinary racegoer, a rank and file punter, is fine up to a point. In fact, it's quite pleasurable just for an afternoon out without the worry and pressure you feel if you have a runner of your own. However, after a while, you want to get back into the fray. I certainly did anyway, so I must have well and truly caught the ownership bug and once you have caught it there is no cure. It is in you for life, I think.

What to do then? Well, I had long admired one other National Hunt trainer of the time and that trainer was John Upson, who trained in Northamptonshire and was noted for producing some really nice, in fact top-class, three-mile chasers. He'd had Sunny Bay in the first part of the horse's career and then, notably, he had trained Nick the Brief who was famous for running Desert Orchid to a neck in a handicap once. He had also run in a Gold Cup and was absolute high class. So I telephoned John one day to see if there were any shares available in any of his horses. There weren't immediately, he said, but he would let me know when there was. After not too long a wait I had a phone call from someone, an Irishman obviously from his accent, called Danny. He ran a partnership at John's which had just acquired a new horse. His stable name was Peter and he was unraced. He was a five-year old and not too far off his first run. He was going to make a chaser one day. Did I want to come down and have a look?

Of course I did. As I said, I had admired John Upson's horses for some time. I liked the fact that he was a pure National Hunt trainer – no flat horse in sight – whose aim was to get all his horses chasing as soon as he could. And I thought being based where he was, I might get to go to some race courses other than those I was by now familiar with on the Northern Circuit. Peter turned out to be a big, strapping chestnut gelding with 'attitude' and he had just been named 'Gaining Ground'. I paid my money to cover the purchase price and signed up there and then at John's stables. John had, actually, been forced to downsize a year or two earlier and had moved down the road to a smaller facility. His biggest owner had turned up one day unannounced with horseboxes and removed his string to another yard. Charlie Brookes' actually. He had just set up as a trainer and John's main owner was a big friend of his. With half his horses gone, literally overnight, John decided to relocate and cut his cloth accordingly. So he was, in fact, now a much smaller trainer than in what you may have called his heyday. But it was a nice, friendly little setup. Danny was a good guy and I was made to feel welcome by all.

Sadly, Gaining Ground seemed to have multiple problems, all of which I cannot now recall. We all knew he wasn't likely to do well in his novice hurdles. He definitely looked like a chaser, but he didn't disgrace himself. His greatest claim to fame actually came in his very first race, I seem to remember. I couldn't get to the meeting because Wincanton is an awfully long way away and I did have to go to work sometimes. But we all noticed that he was to be up against a Paul Nicholls-trained horse, also making his hurdles debut, called Denman. He came into the race with a tremendous reputation after a couple of point-to-points and he was a long odds-on favourite. Peter's sixth or seventh, beaten only about thirty lengths by Denman, a future Gold Cup winner, would turn out to be brilliant form on the face of it, but that performance was probably about as good as it got.

He did go chasing the following season but damaged a knee jumping and I do know that it was always a struggle to keep him fit and sound. After a year or two at the most I, regretfully, decided to come out of the partnership.

I think I was not feeling quite so flush at the time either, on a personal level. Business was getting tougher (I was self-employed and selling into schools) and I didn't seem to be getting the same buzz from this partnership as I had down at Foulrice Farm (Peter Beaumont's yard).

So for a time I was horseless again and I really went through a short phase of thinking I might not bother to become involved again. It was a short phase though and it was a chance meeting with Peter (the trainer, that is not the horse) that made my mind up to become re-involved at some point.

I was going into Wetherby racecourse using the 'back door' or 'tradesman's entrance' to avoid the queues. I don't know if you were supposed to go in that way, as I suspect I was coming in what was meant to be the exit. If I was being naughty I do now hereby repent and apologise to the Wetherby authorities. However, entering by that route took me past the horsebox park and who should I see but none other than Peter Beaumont with his travelling head girl, Sally. I stopped, got out of the car and had a word with him. I guess I had not seen him for at least a year and, as always, he greeted me warmly as he did everyone with his usual phrase, 'Now then'. As we chatted for a while he at some point asked me 'When do you think you might be coming back to us?' and at that instant I thought 'Oh God yes. Would it not be lovely to be back involved again at Peters'?' I think I probably resolved there and then that I would be back again at some point in time.

That point proved not to be so very far off. It came when my wife and I decided to go up to Foulrice Farm just to see Peter and his horses one day. We knew we would be welcomed and it was always an enjoyable day out to go and watch the horses working and see what new arrivals he had. I must point out that we hadn't gone there with any intention of actually buying a horse. I hadn't the money for one thing and, even if I had, how could I afford the running costs? I was doing a bit better again now in my work. I was by this time well-established in the role of sales manager in the educational sales field but a sole racehorse owner I certainly could not be. We simply went up there to watch his horses working, have a chat and possibly at the back of my mind was the thought that I may be able to join another syndicate.

Then, I think just before we were thinking of leaving, Peter dropped out that 'I've got a nice big grey horse in the field. I've not long bought him out of Len Lungo's yard. I'll show him to you if you want. I quite like him.'

So out into the paddocks we went and were introduced to a lovely, broad-chested grey with a nice amount of bone. His name was Rose D'April. Slightly feminine-sounding, I thought, for a gelding. He was seven years old and, we discovered, had run in mid-division in the Champion Bumper race at the Cheltenham Festival previously. He had then won a couple of novice hurdles (ironically beating our Stripe in doing so on one occasion). So we had seen him run before without realising it and the name had, vaguely, rung a bell. Last season he had just started novice chasing before his owners, the Edinburgh Woollen Mill, decided to downsize their string. Peter had recently bought him for £15,000 from Doncaster sales and here we were. We both loved the look of him, and then Peter turned to me and said, 'I haven't got an owner for him yet but if you like we could run him together. You and me. Just put in whatever you can afford and we could work something out. That would be all right with me.'

Suddenly the possibility of owning even a small part of a lovely-looking horse that had been capable of running at the Cheltenham Festival became a reality. After all, there was Rose D'April (stable name Billy) standing in front of us munching grass in all his glory and being offered to me. My mind must have gone into overdrive because I know I was thinking immediately along the lines of 'Who else do I know who might want to share in this horse to help me out?' But the very thought of being able to race him, trained by Peter, made it already a done deal in my head. It was too good an opportunity to miss. My wife, Liz, agreed and, after all, Peter did say 'Just put in what you can afford.'

I can't remember if we actually shook hands on the deal there and then, but I do know that night I drew up a list of people from our previous syndicate and also others from other syndicates at Peter's who I had come across and for whom I had contact details. The next day I was on the phone to them and by close of play a brand new syndicate to run Rose D'April was a definite runner.

I honestly can't remember the number of people I got involved originally, but it was certainly into double figures and there was a lot of enthusiasm for the horse.

Very swiftly the 'Fellowship of the Rose Partnership' was born formed by yours truly in October 2004. At that time a group of co-owners up to twenty was called a 'partnership', and if you had more co-owners than that, up to 100, it was termed a syndicate. More recently the terminology has been changed by the British Horseracing Authority (BHA) so, nowadays, we would be known as a 'syndicate'. Then we were a 'partnership'. Got it? It's just semantics, I know, but whatever they wanted to call us I found myself as the leader of a happy and expectant bunch of jump-racing enthusiasts all pinning their faith on Rose D'April, and, frighteningly, probably me as well. The name of the group actually came a little later when we were formally registered at the BHA. What would we call ourselves? I am never very good at naming things – horses or syndicates – but one of our band came up with the Fellowship of the Rose. The 'rose' part is an obvious reference to our horse's name and the rest, apparently, was a literary allusion. He remembered it from a book he had recently been reading, but I've never been able to recall the actual book or the author. Was it possibly JRR Tolkien? It was just that everyone seemed to think it had a good ring about it. They all liked it. It was a unanimous decision so I registered it. Seventeen-and-a-half years later I am pleased to report that we still exist, although I am the only founder member still in it. Other people have come and gone, as have many horses, but the name lives on even if it is not exactly a household name.

Billy hadn't done a lot of work when we acquired him, so Peter's first task was to get him fit and ready to race. From field to racecourse you can say it will take around thirteen weeks. So it would probably be around the middle to end of January 2005 when he would be scheduled to make his debut for us.

There was tremendous anticipation all around and I recall going up to Peter's not too long before Billy's scheduled first run for us to watch him being schooled over the practice fences by jockey Russ Garrity. He winged them beautifully and Russ and Patrick (the assistant trainer) both said how much they were looking forward to taking him to some nice Saturday meetings at places like Haydock. This was a horse rated just under the 120 mark after all over hurdles and he looked much more of a chasing type. So we were all looking forward to his debut with bated breath.

A little time later I happened to be in a motorway services car park somewhere on the M1 and going about my daily business when the phone call from Peter came. Now Peter, though a marvellous trainer and marvellous man, was not the world's greatest communicator. I, as the owner, always had to phone him. It just didn't seem to happen the other way around. Please do not get me wrong, every time I did phone and get through to him he always had all the time in the world for me and would willingly and honestly keep me up to date but, I think, either by accident or by policy he never instigated the conversation by calling me. Until this time.

It was, quite frankly, difficult to take in. It was bad news. Billy had been turned out the previous day into a paddock on his own and separated by electric fencing from the other horses, following his normal morning's work. They did this a couple of times a week, so nothing out of the ordinary. He then somehow must have slipped and fallen, perhaps having a buck or a frisk or something, no one knew. The first anyone knew was when Patrick from all the way down at the stables heard a tremendous roaring and bellowing from Billy's turnout field. He rushed up there and there he discovered him on the ground, roaring like a lion, in excruciating pain. Patrick and Peter, in all their combined years of experience, had never come across anything like this before. The vet was called. Billy had to be put down out of his agony. When he fell he had broken his breast bone. It was a freak accident. Horses – so tough and yet so fragile at the same time, as I have said.

I was trying to take this all in and, needless to say, was shocked. Peter himself sounded pretty traumatised by the whole affair. And now suddenly we were horseless and the beautiful Rose D'April was gone and he had never even raced for us.

I do remember Peter saying something along the lines of, 'I'll see you all right with another horse. I've got a young gelding you could have.' But that, at that precise time, was hardly the point.

They talk about the ups and downs of horse racing, but this was my first real 'down'. Believe me, a horse unseating at the last fence with the race at his mercy, whilst frustrating and annoying, is not a 'down'. Not set against this. I know I was in a daze for the rest of the day and, of course, I had to tell everyone. First my wife, who I immediately phoned, and then all the other thirteen or fourteen owners at the time (we had grown into a big group). It was not a pleasant duty, repeating the grim news so many times and registering the other people's shock, but it had to be done.

That short chapter of Rose D'April had closed in the most tragic of ways but mostly people in the syndicate stood fast. We retained the same name of the Fellowship of the Rose, in his honour, and Peter, of course, did find us another horse. Meanwhile a framed photograph of Billy still hangs on our dining room wall and I still occasionally reflect on what might have been.

Just My Pal

The next horse (which was, of course, a gift horse) did not quite work out as we had hoped. Peter gave us one of his homebred store horses. He was unnamed and either four or five when we acquired him. He had been backed but not got fit so, inevitably, there was a wait of months, perhaps four or even five, before he was ready to race, so keeping members of the syndicate interested and committed was all important. First, there was a competition to name him. Each member could suggest a name or names and then we all had a vote. You could cast one vote for any name, except ones you had suggested yourself. The new gelding was by Rakaposhi King out of Peter's own broodmare I'm Fine. She was the mare that had produced dear old Stripe. In the end he was officially named 'I'm Posh', which was probably not the most imaginative name but a safe sort of name nevertheless. Unfortunately, I'm Posh turned out not to have too many gears. In fact, I don't think he had any. He was nowhere in a bumper at Huntingdon and then even more adrift in a novice hurdle. The signs were not too good and then, when he somehow managed to escape the confines of his paddock one day when he was turned out and decided to go for a gallop up the tarmac surface of the driveway onto the road, that turned out to be that. He had jarred himself up very badly and his back needed extensive treatment from a physio and a chiropractor. His return to the track looked a very distant possibility. After consulting with Peter, we decided the best thing was to draw a line under I'm Posh and find another horse. He was retired as a riding horse which, in hindsight was probably his true niche in life and the kindest and best thing to do for him.

Meanwhile, most of the syndicate still stuck together. Real racing people are eternal optimists because, I guess, they have to be, and Peter brokered us a deal on what we hoped sounded to be an altogether better proposition.

He (Peter) was friends with a lady called Judy Plummer who had had a horse or two in training at Foulrice Farm previously. She had bred a nice-looking bay colt (who was now gelded) by Paris House out of her own mare. He was four and a nice mover. Judy couldn't quite afford the training fees so she split the ownership with our partnership, thus making him an affordable prospect for both parties.

Again there was a hiatus between acquiring the horse and him running, but patience is a virtue, or so we are told, and we must have been very virtuous folk. Judy did reserve the right to name him, however, so no little naming contest this time around. She named him Just My Pal because, as she explained to me, JMP were her initials and also because he was her pal. He was a thoroughly nice lad too, and he did obviously have some ability. You could see that from the way he moved on the gallops. There was that touch of class about him.

Eventually he was to make his debut in a bumper at Haydock. One or two people in the partnership were becoming ever so slightly impatient but Peter liked to take his time with young horses and get them just right before they ran. I think, being under a bit of pressure myself, I subconsciously in turn put some pressure on Peter to run the horse before he was absolutely ready. I know that Patrick thought he was running him about a month too soon, but, nevertheless, he was entered for Haydock. This would have been the end of February 2005 and Just My Pal would have just turned five. I remember that Peter had another, more fancied runner, in the field. And I also remember our horse running a cracking race to finish a pretty close-up fifth place and that was, as Peter admitted, without being fully wound up. We were delighted, particularly as Peter's other horse in the race finished well behind us and it was owned by none other than that man Trevor Hemmings again. It honestly looked as though we had finally got ourselves a horse we could have some fun and success with at, maybe, a reasonably high level.

There was a slight wait before he raced again. Only until 2 April though. That was enough time to get the horse fully wound up and on that date off we all went to Bangor-on-Dee. Bangor is a lovely country course in a few different ways. The most noticeably quirky thing about it is the fact that you cannot get side on to the winning post, as I have already mentioned. You have to watch the end of the race front on from a grass bank, which serves as a kind of grandstand. The only side-on, conventional view of the winning post that you can get is by watching the big screen. Thank goodness for big screens everywhere. They are now ubiquitous. Whatever did we do before the invention of the big screen? Anyway, Bangor, a lovely place to go racing, especially with the beautiful Welsh hills away to your left and the feel of a real National Hunt course.

We were there for the bumper, of course, which was the last race on the card. And, although there was a red-hot favourite for the race called Arnold Layne, I think we were quite hopeful he would give another good account of himself. All was going well enough as he settled in mid-division on the first circuit and he was travelling as well as anything approaching the enclosures for the first time. Then it all went horribly wrong. A horse (as it happened, trained by Sue Smith, wife of legendary show jumper Harvey) veered suddenly across the track from the rails side. It had obviously caught sight of the stables to his right and wanted to get back to them pretty quickly. He ploughed across the course

Just My Pal

straight through the rest of the field causing mayhem. He hampered plenty of other horses but, as he crashed across, must have somehow clipped our lad on the lower part of his leg somewhere around the fetlock. Going around the bend away from the enclosure our jockey looked down and immediately pulled up. When he jumped off and started looking at one of the horse's forelegs we knew there was a big problem. He was obviously injured and lame but we didn't know yet to what extent. But the sight of the horse ambulance going round to recover him filled us with foreboding.

When Just My Pal did make it back in the ambulance to the racecourse stables it became rapidly clear the seriousness of his injury. I can't now remember the name of the exact bone that he had broken, but it was a small one in or around the fetlock. It was a small one but big enough to mean that the vet could tell me straight away that he would never race again. When he announced that it was a hammer blow. What a lovely horse. What a bright future he had and now there was no future for him. No future for him on the racecourse, at least.

Judy was very good about the whole thing, although she must have been even more heartbroken than we were, having bred him and seen him every day of his life. He was the apple of her eye, but she had been around horses long enough, I guess, to know all the pitfalls. All the few highs and all the seemingly many lows. He was taken to a local vet initially and then transported to a vet close to Judy. The prognosis was that if he could be immobilised in his box as much as possible for the next few months, he might recover sufficiently to at least live out his natural life in her field as a companion or something. We all hoped and prayed that this would be the case but, in the end, it was not to be. It was clear that after a period of several weeks there was very little progress and he was still in a lot of pain. He had to have an awful lot of bute (painkillers) in his system all the time and eventually Judy took the decision to do the right thing by him. And so Just My Pal was put down at home where he had been born, and the curtain dropped on another episode in my racehorse-owning life.

Pinch Me Silver

There were times I really felt like giving up the whole project and this was one of them. Nothing seemed to have gone right since I formed the partnership. And yet optimism always got the better of me and, after all, there is always the next time.

Peter wanted to keep us in the yard as well and trainers feel as bad as owners about the loss of a horse. After all, they see them and handle them every day. We, as owners, only see them at the racecourse or intermittently in between. So he offered us another gift horse. In fact, it was Patrick who suggested we should take on Patty.

Patty was a nice young bay (again). A mare by Silver Patriarch, who had won the St. Leger, and bred a lot of good National Hunt horses. She was out of a mare called Pinch, who had only raced once for Nicky Henderson. What a lovely-looking horse Patty was though and not too far off having her first run too. So the remaining partners kept the faith and Patty became ours. This time Peter wanted to name her himself. Perhaps he hadn't liked our choice of I'm Posh previously. I'm not sure. However, pretty soon Patty became Pinch Me Silver, a name which I always thought made her sound as if she should have been a grey.

Her debut, which was at my local track of Uttoxeter, turned out to be surrounded by drama. It was, by now, midsummer and so the summer racing programme was in full swing. At the end of June, Uttoxeter hosted (and still does) a meeting with a big, valuable steeplechase as its focus. At the time it was called the

English Summer National although now its distance has been cut back and it has had several renamings. Patty was to have her first run in the bumper, the final race on the card. It was a warm summer's day and we were expecting a large turnout of partners because many were pretty local. I had recruited a local fellow called Derek who was disabled and not in the best of health anyway, but he had always had a passion for racing. His dream had been to own a racehorse and now, finally, before it was too late he had decided to go for it and have a share in Patty. He was not a wealthy man by any means and so a syndicate is tailored made for someone in his position. Elaborate plans were made by friends to drive him to the course and get him into the parade ring in his wheelchair and I know how much he was really looking forward to the day. He couldn't travel very far but Uttoxeter was only ten miles away and he could make that okay in his friend's car.

The first drama was that there was a massive pileup on the A50, the road that they had to take to get to Uttoxeter, and they were caught up in a seemingly interminable tailback. I and other partners were safely at the course by then but Derek had left it late so that he could get there about halfway through the meeting, as a whole day at the races would have been too much for him to cope with. So I received urgent phone calls and texts during the course of the afternoon letting me know of their progress, or lack of it.

Then the second drama occurred. I was aware of some activity in the space between the two stands but wasn't sure what was happening. Then someone told me they thought there was a fire in a mobile betting shop down in that direction, but there didn't seem to be any kind of a panic about it and so I assumed someone had grabbed a fire extinguisher and that the incident was over. Oh no! This small fire had grown into a larger one and then continued to get larger. Large enough to catch the end of the main stand in fact. There was an announcement to evacuate the stand, which everyone did immediately. Then another announcement to say that the next race had been delayed – no surprise there. Another announce-ment told us that the fire brigade had been called and were on their way and, just for everyone's safety, could the crowd please make its way across the course into the centre course enclosures. Everyone of course complied and there, from the centre of the course, you could suddenly gain a view of what looked to me like spectacularly dangerous flames lapping up the side of the main grandstand. The mobile betting shop was by now a burned out shell!

The fire brigade arrived, the next race was put back even further and I was beginning to think that there was no chance of racing continuing at all. A phone call came in from Derek. They were still stuck in a traffic jam and he was starting to feel unwell and, assuming racing would be abandoned for the day anyway, they were going to turn back and go home at the first available opportunity. Derek's dream had been ruined and, sadly, he never made it to the parade ring as an owner. Other racecourses were too distant for him and about a year later he passed away, an ambition unfulfilled.

Meanwhile, at Uttoxeter we were treated, if that is the correct word, to an expert display of fire-fighting by the Staffordshire Fire Brigade and, eventually, after what seemed a very long time, the fire was out and the area made safe enough, miraculously, for racing to resume and for the crowd to be let back onto some of the stands.

The downside was that we were now running about two and a half hours late, meaning Patty, instead of running in the 5:15, was now in the revised 7:45! It was amazing that the race was run at all. I had earlier abandoned all hope of it going ahead. But it was a run, and Patty on her debut finished an honourable third to a horse who was really a flat-bred horse and who was a hot odds-on favourite. It had never run on the flat, of course, but later it did so and, although it won another bumper, it never did have a jumping career. Its trainer was really just misusing the bumper system to win some easy prize money.

Patty ran okay in another bumper and then went novice hurdling. She did pretty well in a novice hurdle at Ayr, which I couldn't get to. She finished a respectable sixth and it boded well for future handicaps. She also had races at Bangor and then Kelso where, on both occasions, she gave a good account of herself, although she was just out of the prize money. It seemed from these performances that we may well have a reasonable sort of horse. No great star, but like all of Peter's horses, one that would improve when it went over fences. That was the aim for her and we were all looking forward to her steeplechasing debut the following autumn.

She was scheduled to be schooled over fences during the summer and all seemed to be going according to plan. She jumped well and we all thought she would probably be up to 20 lbs better over fences compared to hurdles. However, I well remember another fateful telephone conversation that I had with Peter. This time it was the very day before Patty was due to make her chasing debut at Carlisle. At that time she could bypass a novice chase and go straight into a handicap on her hurdle ratings so expectations were high. As soon as I saw it was Peter calling I somehow feared the worst. There was something wrong, otherwise he would not be phoning me when we were due to be at Carlisle in the morning. He explained that Patty, just that morning (why she had been galloping the day before a race I still don't know) had broken down on her off fore and broken down quite badly. It wasn't a small injury. She would not be running tomorrow, he said and, to be honest, I feared from the general tone of his voice that she would not be running for a very long time if, in fact, ever again.

Oh my God. Another big belt in the solar plexus. As always, as leader of this happy band, I had to then repeat the message over and over and explain the situation. It was not an easy nor comfortable thing to do. More stress – and this was supposed to be a fun hobby for all concerned. Again, I remember the exact car park I happened to be in when Peter delivered this shock to the system. And did I think of packing the whole thing in now and saying 'to hell with it'? Well no. For whatever reasons I never did consider doing that although, I suspect, there would have been those who wouldn't have blamed me.

After this sad event Peter did offer us a couple of other horses on a lease basis but they didn't work out. The memory of both has almost faded completely. Neither did anything at all for us, although I would never blame Peter for offering these horses. One was called Stan the Man and he was absolutely huge. He was chestnut and probably 17 hands high, but he had problems, maybe because he was so big. He was never going to be a hurdler as we found out after his first run and then he began to develop all sorts of physical problems. It became obvious he would never become a long-term prospect and he was, therefore, duly abandoned by us to become another riding horse. The other one, sad to say, I cannot even recall now and I'm not sure if he ever got to the racecourse for us. Effectively, that was the end of our period with the wonderful Peter Beaumont.

Peter retired officially about a year later, but, by the summer of 2009 I decided we had to move on to another trainer because things just weren't the same at Foulrice Farm. Peter seemed to be running things down and at seventy-five he had maybe lost some of his energy for the job. It had been a tremendous time and, although I had personally experienced just the two winners, it felt like we had also had the privilege of being involved with the Gold Cup winner, and RSA Chase winner, a Scottish and Midland Grand National winners and many others too. We had also had the privilege of being involved with a truly great trainer and one of the most respected men ever in racing. Sadly, it was time to move on and the thought of never seeing horses galloping around Foulrice Farm again was hard to imagine at the time.

I am so pleased and proud to say that Peter and I stayed in touch after our departure and we would pop up to see him on the farm or at Easingwold, where he later lived, and have another really good chat about racing, life and everything else. His death in March 2020 came as a blow to me and many, many others but was not altogether unexpected because he had become very frail in his last few years. He was so kind and fair to all his owners and as genuinely pleased to see and to talk to a small syndicate owner like myself as a large multi-horse owner who was contributing a lot more to his bank balance. He was a real horseman, a real stockman who had a brilliant eye for a good horse and he knew how to treat them and train them well. He had started in the point-to-point field so was a real National Hunt man and he told me repeatedly that his one regret was that he hadn't taken out a full licence earlier. He would have been about fifty-two when he got his first full licence. Some trainers are thinking about retirement when they reach that age! Yet he still had sufficient time to train all those great horses plus loads of other, ordinary ones like ours, all to their optimum. What a great fellow. All I can say is, from the bottom of my heart, thank you Peter Beaumont. I suspect there may be a few others who would join me in expressing that sentiment.

It was going to have to be the start of a new era. I was left with a small, loyal rump of supporters who seemed willing to follow me anywhere, but probably not enough of them to support a whole racehorse.

By now the racing bug was so strong with me that I knew, whatever, I had to keep the whole thing going. I just could not do without the buzz. So I consulted with the loyal leftovers, if I may call them that, and decided to seek out an alternative trainer so that, somehow, we could carry on racing.

Business Class
and Ritsi

It was late summer in 2009 by now and I thought I would check out some trainers that, for one reason or another, I thought might be okay for us. They obviously had to be jumps trainers and also be flexible in their approach. I needed someone who would be willing to do us a 'deal' and not someone who just stated their daily rate for training, take it or leave it. So I set out on an odyssey to find a future trainer.

I did some research myself and was also recommended a trainer close to Peter's by another of his former owners who had moved there. I thought I would go and check them all out. I undertook a tour of some trainers. One was local to me, the others were in North Yorkshire. The local guy (I won't mention any names here) was, in fact, a really nice husband-and-wife team who had trained one or two decent winners in their time. They were unfortunate in that their main owner, if they ever acquired a really good horse with whom they had some success, would send it off then to Nicky Henderson or a trainer of similar stature. When I went to see them they were just going through a lean time. They no longer train, having finished a few years ago. As nice as they were, they were unfortunately completely unimaginative and inflexible. They had a fixed price for training per day and were not interested in doing deals whereby, for instance, they would retain a proportion of the horse if the prospective owner could not afford their full fees. It was take it or leave it and so I had no choice but to leave it. I did not have enough committed owners to take on a whole horse and then guarantee the monthly training fees. I guess other potential owners at the time (remember this was at the start of the recession) had similar problems and with their rigid approach it must have contributed to these trainers' demise, which was a big shame.

The second trainer was suggested by one of our owners merely because he taught his son at a rather expensive public school. It was an interesting morning out but it was obvious he was out of our league. He was only really interested in wealthy owners and expensive horses. He didn't cater for the likes of us on a budget so that was a blank.

My last trip, also in North Yorkshire, was to a village a few miles away from Peter's. Marjorie Fife had only been training for a year or two and she (along with husband Will and son Tom) had that flexible approach that I was looking for. They were looking to increase the number of horses they had in training and were more than willing to retain any unsold portions of a horse. They seemed, at first meeting, a nice enough family and the set up was okay. These were the people recommended to us by the former owner at Peter Beaumont's. Stables were at the back of the family bungalow and they had use of a larger trainer's gallops a few miles away. I discovered that Marjorie was quite progressive in her training methods and did a lot of interval training rather than out-and-out galloping. It was a system brought over from her eventing days and entailed horses doing short bursts of work for a set number of minutes, followed by a set number of minutes of recovery time. There is more than one road to Rome, as they say, and she could get horses fit. She had already trained winners under both codes.

So I reported back to my remaining band of owners (referred to now by Liz as my 'acolytes') and it was unanimously agreed to ask Marjorie Fife to find us a relatively cheap horse. She thought something off the flat to go hurdling with might suit us, even though I had a few personal reservations about this. I prefer the proper chasing types, but I could see the attraction of her plan and so could everyone else. You would be buying a horse who knew how to race, had some speed, wouldn't have to go through the laborious process of running in bumpers and would, most likely, be ready to run immediately, once it had been schooled over hurdles.

The training fees and general terms were agreed upon and so we officially had a new trainer and were all ready to go. All we needed now was a horse.

Rather than go to the sales she would ask about and see what might be available and, after going up one or two blind alleys, she came up with a Brazilian-bred horse called Business Class (very South American!) who had won a race on the all-weather over a mile. Now I always thought that for a flat horse to get the two miles required to go hurdling, it would have to be at the very least a one-mile two-furlong horse. However, I was assured that he would get the trip. I had to have faith. What did I know about it really? It was decided that Business Class, since he was already fit, should have a race or two on the flat anyway prior to him going over jumps, and we all trooped off to Wolverhampton one night (it was now November 2009) full of hopes and expectations. We need not have got excited because our horse, after a keen start, faded and finished nowhere. Ah well, it had been a different experience. Wolverhampton under floodlights with noisy stag and hen parties going on in the bars. And the new horse was supposed to be a hurdler anyway – wasn't he?

He did have another flat race or two without distinguishing himself and then, it was decided, the time was right for him to be schooled and make his hurdling debut. The jumping bit turned out not to be a problem. He took to that well and didn't touch a twig. The problem was that in his first race he faded badly after a bright start, probably about four furlongs out, and finished totally tailed off. We had gone to Huntingdon that day, again full of hope, and were now deflated. But what would the jockey tell us about him when he got back? Phil Kinsella (a very experienced jockey and a good judge of a horse) was on board. He told us straight away and in no uncertain terms that this horse didn't get the trip and never would. He was not a horse for the National Hunt game at all. He was an out-and-out flat horse.

I can remember us all looking at each other aghast in frustration and wonderment after the race that day at Huntington. We were all thinking the same thing. Where do we go from here? We had a flat horse to run over about a mile but I had told everyone we had bought a two-mile jumps horse. It looked as though it was back to the drawing board for us all, although William said afterwards as cheerily as possible, 'Well at least you still have a sound horse that's ready to run. You've got to look on the bright side.' That, sadly, was not the point. That was not what we had bought into. Looking back, I think that buying Business Class had been an attempt by Marjorie to get the type of horse for us that she preferred training. She always said that flat horses were easier to train, stayed sounder and could run more often. All of that is of course true but, again, missed the point. We were a jumps syndicate. I think it was always going to be a bit of a punt on her part as to whether he would stay the two miles. It could have just worked but, anyway, it didn't.

There were three more horses we had with the Fifes over a period of about three years and, to be fair, we had one memorable winning experience over hurdles at Wetherby in June 2012. More of that later, but the other two horses were not a success. They were, at least, proper National Hunt horses but the first was pretty slow and also couldn't stand up to the rigours of racing. He developed very dodgy knees and had to be retired as a riding horse. The next, which we bought out of Howard Johnson's yard when he finished training for a sum certainly in excess of £10,000, had had problems before, and in his second race for us (it was at Catterick) broke down and was never able to run again. He was a lovely big French-bred horse with a hurdles rating of about 120 so, again trying to be fair to Marjorie, he was the stamp we were looking for. I guess it was just bad luck in the end and we seemed to be gaining a reputation for that – bringing bad luck to stables. Sometimes it seemed that way, but it was no good feeling sorry for yourself and, somehow, I kept brushing myself down and kept going, always taking a batch of owners with me. Anyway, I don't really believe in being lucky or unlucky. You make your own luck by being persistent and tenacious. I think it was the great South African golfer Gary Player who said 'It's strange, the more I practise the luckier I get.' How true.

And we did get lucky with the last horse we had at Marjorie's, although even then there was a nasty, sad sting in the tail. The horse was called Ritsi; a loan horse who had been owned by Marjorie's parents. They said he could run under our name after we lost our lovely French horse. Ritsi must have been an eight-year old when we took him over, so pretty experienced. He had won one long distance flat race and had also run over hurdles. He was a proven genuine dual-purpose horse and came with a hurdles rating around 100 – so this time we knew exactly where we stood. He had raced several times for us under both codes, running very respectably without ever threatening to win us anything. Then, at the beginning of June 2012, he was entered for a two-mile hurdle at Wetherby. It was generally thought that Ritsi was much better on softer ground and so running him during the summer jumping season was hardly ideal, but we all wanted to get to the races.

On 6 June that year, however, things went our way for a change. It started raining early in the morning and it just kept coming down all day long in bucketfuls. By the time we got to Wetherby the going turned to heavy. Heavy going in June is a pretty rare occurrence. It wasn't the greatest of races I must admit but he was still sent off at 50 to 1. I thought he should have been a bit shorter than that but we still realistically didn't hold out too much hope for him.

Up to that race I had always made a point of going to the tote or the bookies and having a minimum each-way bet just to show that I had supported our horse. I intended doing so on this occasion – except that the rain was torrential and the betting ring some way away from the parade ring at Wetherby and could I be bothered to become even more drenched just to have a futile bet? No, I decided, I couldn't be bothered. So I went instead to the owners' viewing area in the stand. It was lovely and warm and dry in there.

By now you will have guessed what happened. Ritsi, obviously loving the conditions, ploughed through the Yorkshire mud and as the other horses dropped away one by one, he sluiced through the mire to win by several lengths. The first win for the Fellowship of the Rose Partnership. It was unabated jubilation as I and a small group of our partners that had made it to Wetherby that day raced to greet our new hero back in the winner's enclosure! Then there was the presentation, the photographs and the replay of the race just to make sure it had really happened. That was definitely the zenith of our days with the Fifes and she did have a knack, it must be admitted, of producing from time-to-time an unexpected win out of nothing.

After all the excitement of the day it wasn't until the following day sometime, that I realised that I hadn't actually bothered to put that bet on him. Even my meagre £2.50 each way would have produced a nice £156 profit. And I had not got round to doing it because of a drop of rain. Ah well, it didn't actually matter. It would hardly have been a life-changing amount but the thrill and excitement of the win was irreplaceable and will stay with me (and the others) forever. It really sums up why we do it. We're not in it for the money. Far from it. We want to be involved in racing for all the other non-pecuniary reasons. The horses, the buzz, the drama, the few ups, the many downs, the anticipation, the memories. Perhaps I could add to that list but, as I tell anyone whoever expresses an interest in having a share with us, don't expect to make money out of this. Be prepared to kiss goodbye to your monthly subscription like you would if you joined a gym or a golf club. We're all doing it for the sheer pleasure of being involved with this great sport and its principal participants – the horses.

So we knew now that Ritsi was a soft-ground horse if we hadn't realised it already and Marjorie thought he may stay further and get three miles. She tried him over that three-mile distance at Bangor but he didn't get the trip. He was pulled up with several furlongs to go even though the going was his favoured soft. He continued to race for us for the rest of that year alternating between flat and over hurdles and I remember him getting placed over hurdles a couple of times at Carlisle. I also recall an enjoyable day out on the flat at Doncaster. He finished down in the field but everyone enjoyed going to a major racecourse. Then, right at the start of the new year (2013), came his big chance. A two-mile handicap hurdle at Uttoxeter where conditions had, overnight, become so bad that it was barely raceable. In fact, we were kind of assuming it would be abandoned as it was raining so hard with no sign of abating. However, racing went ahead with horses sloshing around in deep mud. Testing was an understatement. I can't recall his starting price but I made certain to have my each-way bet on him this time!

From our vantage point in the viewing area and also by watching the big screen, all seemed to be going very well indeed in the early stages. He was travelling well. As well as any other horse in the race, and as they turned into the straight for the final time he began to cut through effortlessly. He was relishing these conditions again and, suddenly, it looked like a repeat of Wetherby. Except somewhere about two flights out something happened. The jockey began to look down, the horse faltered in his stride and we knew something was amiss. Suddenly he was pulled up and instantly our expectations of victory and the elation that would have gone with it turned into a stomach-churning foreboding. How serious things were with him we had no idea, but I recall Marjorie and his girl running flat out down the course to him.

Sometime later after trying to find out some news about him, we found Marjorie and William and from the expression on their faces, the news was obviously not going to be good.

I forget the actual name of the injury sustained but it spelled the end of his racing career at the very least. A small bone in his fetlock had been broken. I think it was similar to Just My Pal's.

Did we carry a curse with us? Were we perpetual bad luck? Well, I doubt it. There are, sadly, plenty of injured ex-race horses about and it is a risky sport. We hoped that Ritsi would recover from his injury sufficiently to, at least, spend the rest of his days turned out with a friend in his field eating grass. But it was not to be. As it turned out it was eventually decided that the most humane thing to do was to put him to sleep. How quickly that day at Uttoxeter had turned from a potential 'high' to a rock bottom, depressing 'low'.

After Ritsi it was decision time. Relations had not always been that easy with the trainer, although there were never any fall outs. I don't do 'falling out'. Life is too short. But now running the syndicate, which previously had always been a pleasure despite its challenges, was becoming something of a pain. There were a couple or three members who seemed to have unrealistic expectations and who liked to blame me if the horses put in a poor run. I was increasingly feeling under pressure, which was not the idea of it at all. In addition, earlier in 2012 one of the main parties pulled out at short notice in some fit of pique or other. The partnership was suddenly not what it was and the experience of running it was becoming a chore.

Snow Alert

With Ritsi gone and only a rump of the partners left I thought that this might well be the end of the road for us. However, something kept me going and perhaps I was propelled into keeping going by my last experience at the Fifes.

Marjorie had found a replacement horse for us. It was a horse off the flat who would make a nice hurdler, she said. Sounds familiar? It had been schooled over hurdles at home, I was informed, but was, for whatever reason, for sale privately at a reasonable price. She strongly recommended it.

I was not happy about it though. I just had a gut instinct about it and, although I said I would consult the other partners, I somehow felt that, if we were to keep going at all, it could be time to find another trainer. That, I knew, would not be an easy task, however, because any trainer would have to be prepared to retain a portion of the horse again. If I could not find another trainer willing to take us on with those sort of terms then I had the feeling the partnership would have to be closed down.

In the meantime Marjorie had bought the flat horse for us anyway, as the remaining partners seemed to think it would be a good idea to have him. I reluctantly parted with some money for him, or at least, part of him. I felt that I had got myself into a bit of a mess over this. I was not happy about the situation at all and I felt out of control.

It was then about the end of January or the beginning of February 2013 and I decided to take a positive step without even consulting the other partners. I was going to have a go at finding a new trainer and see if I could extricate myself from this unhappy situation. What we would do with this newly acquired horse if I did find another trainer I had no idea, but I felt I just had to do something. So I went on a trawl of the internet to find details of a trainer I thought might be okay, but they all seemed either too expensive or not prepared to do deals, as it were, with small, hard-up owners. Then, somehow, I happened across the name of a trainer that was reasonably local to me in South Yorkshire and whose rates seemed more affordable. He was only a small trainer, so I thought perhaps he may be more flexible as far as deals were concerned. I knew nothing about the guy except it was a name I had seen on race cards from time-to-time, but I had no idea what sort of reception I would get if I were to phone him up. Anyway, it was the last option so I girded my loins and gave him a call. It proved to be a significant if not life-changing move, as far as my partnership was concerned. The trainer's name was John Richard Norton.

I knew he was based in South Yorkshire in a village called High Hoyland, which I mistook for a place I knew just south of Barnsley, which is just plain Hoyland. He was quick to point out that you shouldn't get the two places confused because High Hoyland was a whole lot more rural on the edge of the Pennines, 900 feet up with views across the lowlands to the east. As soon as I got into conversation on the phone with John I knew we might have every possibility of carrying on as a group. I explained our precarious financial situation and that we were looking for a trainer who would be prepared to share ownership of a horse with us. In his round Barnsley tones he told me 'That's strange because I was just putting pen to paper at this minute to compose an advert for a horse I've got here. He's nearly ready to run and I'd like someone to come in and take some shares in him. I could offer him on a lease as well if you'd like. His name is Snow Alert and he's run in bumpers and is ready to go hurdling.'

Well, I thought, you don't look a gift horse in the mouth, and in any case John sounded so nice and friendly and down to earth that I instantly felt that here was a chap I could really warm to and get on with. It was an instinctive feeling and it proved to be correct.

'Why don't you come up, have a look at him, and we can have a chat, Phil. Maybe do a deal.'

I took him up on his offer and later let the remaining loyal partners know what I was doing. A few days later Liz and I set off up the M1 to Globe Farm to meet John and Snow Alert. As soon as we set foot on his yard we both had positive vibes about the place. It was a small (only about twelve horses in) and scrupulously tidy yard. The horses looked happy, interested and content and there was a general impression of orderliness about the place. John himself and his dad (another John, but John senior) were friendly and welcoming. But the important thing was I knew immediately we were both talking the same language in terms of hammering out a mutually beneficial arrangement together. He offered us a fixed monthly inclusive fee with no hidden extras and suggested splitting the horse 50/50 if I thought that was doable. The horse would be offered on a lease to us so that it meant no capital outlay for the partnership. He didn't put us under any pressure but I felt before we left that the deal was already done as far as I was concerned, and I couldn't envisage any of our band having any objections. There was still the little matter, however, of the horse I had rather stupidly parted money for at the Fifes. What was I going to do about that? I did mention this situation to John before we left and when I told him from which yard it had been purchased he said, 'Well, I know him (the trainer) quite well. Known him for years. I'll give him a call and see what I can find out about this horse and why it was for sale in the first place. If I can help you sort something out I will.'

He did just that and very promptly too, and reported back to me that he had discovered the horse had had knee problems, had never been schooled over hurdles and, although not a bad horse on the flat, they just wanted to get rid. I never did tell Marjorie what I had found out but, nonetheless, I felt emboldened by this newfound knowledge and decided to go back to her, tell her I had found a new yard to go to and ask for my money back. Strangely, it was a request she immediately agreed to. I think she had seen the writing on the wall and she had also found out somehow, on the grapevine, that John had contacted the previous trainer. So an agreement was arrived at. The flat horse became the Fifes' property and Marjorie did say that if it ever won a race for her she would 'see me all right'. The 'seeing all right' was never specified but that was the least of my concerns. Suddenly I got a new surge of liberation and positivity. A big burden had been lifted from my shoulders and I could look forward once again to running a new horse in a new yard with enthusiasm. What is more, all the remaining partners were fully on board. The dissenters had gone and from that date in early February 2013 until the present, all have remained on board and totally loyal both to me and to John. Stress in running this partnership was to become a thing of the past. By the way, the flat horse did win a race (on the flat of course) and several weeks later, true to her word, I was 'seen all right'. A bottle of Bell's Scotch Whisky was posted to me and duly and gratefully accepted.

Snow Alert, meanwhile, was by now a seven-year-old chestnut gelding who had only been lightly raced. He had shown, as the Racing Post is apt to put it, a glimmer of ability. It has to be said that he was a bit lean and unremarkable-looking at first sight. He was possibly big enough to take a fence one day but the immediate aim was a novice hurdling career. It was thought he probably favoured the better ground so if he was ready to race in March it would coincide, with a bit of luck, with his preferred ground. In his bumpers and his one novice hurdle so far he had, as I said, only shown perhaps a glimmer of ability but John said that, whilst he would never be a star, he had the right attitude and should give us all some fun.

Well, Snow Alert (who rapidly became known as 'Snowy') did just that despite some hiccups. I remember inexplicably bad runs at Southwell and Catterick but otherwise he gave a good account of himself in novice hurdles without ever getting himself placed. But when he got his handicap mark he, obviously, became a lot more competitive and although he remained forever a maiden he did win us odd bits of prize money.

It just occurred to me that in the last sentence I used the word 'maiden' as if I assumed that everyone reading this would automatically know what I meant. It is, of course, another piece of racing jargon (meaning a horse that has never won a race) and therefore I have made a mental note to try and explain these terms as they may crop up. I take them for granted now, but I accept they may be confusing to many. Personally, I have always loved the arcane terminology and jargon of the racing industry. Racing these days is always trying to make itself more 'accessible' to the wider public but I think one of its great charms is that despite in essence being a very simple sport, it has all these complexities that you have to work out. There is one publication called the Rules of Racing and a very weighty tome it is indeed and not recommended bedtime reading. It illustrates, however, just how thoroughly the sport is governed down to the most minute detail. And trainers are expected at all times to conform to these rules and be fully aware of them all (and any changes that have been brought in). However, I find it fascinating. If a thing is too straightforward and simple, surely it becomes boring? Racing is never that. Back to Snowy – he raced for us for just over a year with, as I say, mixed fortunes, but he was always a genuine trier and had a handicap rating somewhere in the 80s. But his career ended at Uttoxeter in May 2014 when, after he came in a really game and close-up third in a handicap hurdle, we could instantly see as he walked into the winner's enclosure that he was quite badly lame in front.

It looked pretty bad and immediately I had a thought that it was shades of Ritsi – and the same course as well. My local course. It turned out, in fact, to be a tendon injury which would, in the fullness of time (about a year), heal itself. However, by the time he was got fit again and ready to race you could easily be talking about an eighteen-month delay. In addition, once a horse has had a bad tendon injury there is always that possibility of it recurring, particularly in jumps horse with a lot of pressure coming down on front legs as they land over the obstacles. So it was decided between us and John that the best course of action would be to get Snowy sound again and then sell him onto someone as a riding horse whilst we would acquire a new horse. Snowy did, in fact, eventually go to a lovely lady bus driver from Sheffield who wanted to use him as a hack and general fun horse so, thankfully, he had a very happy and safe retirement.

Racehorses give us so much on the racecourse and so I firmly believe that it is, therefore, our duty as owners to make sure they go to the best possible home once their career is over. I shall return to that subject later anyway.

Fiddler's Flight

Meanwhile, the other problem was the acquisition of a new horse. Would that mean putting our hands in our pockets again? Could folk afford it? What sum were people prepared to part with? Luckily, none of those questions needed to be answered thanks to John, who phoned me up and said, 'I've got this horse in the yard that might just be okay for you.' Prophetic words they were too, because he was referring to Fiddler's Flight – or Joe to his friends. Again we split him 50/50 with John and, after a quick check with my remaining fellow partners, we were in business again.

At this point I think it is probably appropriate to give a few details about my co-owners because it was at this point that the partnership settled down and became a group of really reliable and committed people. Running the syndicate was now a pleasure with no comings and goings, no moanings about this and that. And when we met up at the races it was now a group of friends meeting for a day out. I also started to feel appreciated by them all for the work I was putting in to keep the show on the road and get a horse we could have fun with. Running a racehorse syndicate, no matter how small or humble, is not an easy or straightforward task and keeping all the people happy all the time is well-nigh impossible if you have a few truculent individuals who probably think they could do a better job but, of course, would never have the oomph even to try.

Well now the scenario was different: a group of seven (including myself) sensible and enthusiastic people who just wanted days out racing, a horse to follow and no unrealistic expectations.

So to our group. There was Pat, an accountant now retired, from Wilmslow in Cheshire. Adam owned and ran a pub in Derby. Chrissie ran (along with her husband Tim) a company that raised funds for a charity. She was from Preston. Diane and Marion, who respectively are my niece and older sister, who lived in Derby but then moved to Burton-upon-Trent. Finally Colin, also from Derby, although a Welshman by birth. He had been mine and Liz's financial adviser for some years. He had had a share in a nice horse at Nigel Twiston-Davies' stables some years before and was a real racing aficionado. His company also had been sponsoring our horse which, as I'll explain later, is very important to any racing syndicate.

Of the others, Pat and Adam had both been with me since the Peter Beaumont days and were both knowledgeable racing people. Pat had been a member at Haydock for many years and was an inveterate race goer. Adam liked having a bet and following the form. Chrissie didn't know too much about racing but was a horse fan and soon got into the excitement of ownership. And my niece (who is keen on all sorts of sports) and sister just enjoy the interest and buzz of ownership, not to mention the free hospitality at racecourses. They are there for the good runs and the bad, to sample the food, which thankfully all courses offer owners now, and mark them out of 10.

That was my happy band of followers or, as Liz termed them, my 'acolytes'. Now for our new horse – the one who was to give us our biggest thrills and most memorable moments so far, even though he was never a big star within the horse racing firmament. But he turned out to be and will forever remain our 'big star'. Let's begin at the beginning with Fiddler's Flight. He was bred in Northern Ireland on 12 May 2006 by Joe Magee – hence his stable name of Joe. He was by a stallion called

Convinced out of a mare called Carole's Dove, who in turn was related to a mare that had won the Champion Hurdle some years before – Flakey Dove. So he was not a badly bred horse at all.

However, this is not a tale of how an ordinary little horse with ordinary little owners soared to great heights. If you look back on his racing career record with a dispassionate eye it looks pretty unspectacular. No unexpected Aintree or Cheltenham heroics for him but that only proves that in racing you don't have to be at the top of the tree to get all the thrills. I bet Joe gave us more excitement than all of JP McManus's put together. Let's start with Joe Magee. I never did have the chance to meet him because, sadly, he had died of cancer just as Fiddler's Flight was making his racecourse debut, but he was, apparently, a colourful and not untypical breeder of thoroughbreds in Northern Ireland. He had a farm full of them and had sent a few over the years to John's to be trained. If they had a bit of success with one in a bumper, for instance, they would sell it on and split the profit. It was that kind of relationship. One day John received a phone call from Joe telling him about this now six-year old horse he had who was a bit out of control and wild. Could John take him and see if he could do anything with him?

Well, John Norton is not one to duck a challenge and so he said, 'Yes, send him over and I'll see what I can do.'

It transpired that this so called 'out of control' horse had, in fact been backed at three and then turned away for, supposedly, a year to mature. Actually that year had then turned into three because Joe Magee had forgotten about his existence. Hardly surprising therefore that the then unnamed Fiddlers Flight was a bit resentful and unprepared for the constraints of work when, eventually, they had rescued him from the field.

He was duly shipped over during the winter of 2012–13 and, for various logistical reasons John arranged with the transporter to take delivery of him in the lorry park at Sedgefield racecourse, a place that would become very well known to the horse later.

Then the fun began. Joe was never the easiest horse to train. He was very sharp and took pleasure in ditching his rider off if he could. He was also a fussy eater who had to be tempted. Getting him to eat up his 15 pounds of corn a day was a major feat in itself. But he was okay in the stable and, despite his nervy exterior, he was a nice enough chap underneath. However, he didn't seem the type that would switch off and settle in a race and, because of his relatively advanced age when he came into training, he was not eligible to run in bumpers to get a bit of practice in that department. He would just have to be pitched into novice hurdles straight away.

Eventually, though, he was ready to make his debut in October of 2013. John and his father, John Norton Senior, were still the co-owners at that point and so they, of course, had chosen his name. The first choice name had, in fact, been Fiddler's Elbow but that name had already been taken so John's dad had come up with the alliterative 'Flight' as an alternative. We were running Snow Alert at the time so we didn't really register that he finished a respectable fifth of eight at Southwell in his first novice hurdle. The first time I was really aware of Joe was during the April of the following year. He had been given the rest of the winter off so it was only his second race and he was running against his stablemate Snow Alert in a two-and-a-half mile maiden hurdle at Wetherby. Snowy finished sixth or seventh in a big field but I do remember Fiddler's Flight hurtling off, barely in control, and then about halfway through the race nosediving over a hurdle and, apparently unseating his jockey, although it was given officially as a fall. I also remember John saying after that race that, in his opinion, he thought Fiddler's Flight might turn out to be a better horse than Snow Alert if he could only get him to calm down and settle.

Just over a month later, at the end of May 2014, Joe was to come into our ownership because of Snowy's injury at Uttoxeter. And that was to be the real start of our journey with him.

In a way we were off to a bit of a false start with him because John was just giving him a few weeks' break. He was munching grass at High Hoyland in his paddock. The plan was to get him back in fairly soon as it was only planned as a mini-break. He should be fit to run again by the end of August, ground permitting, when the 'proper' jump season had got going again.

We did go up to have a look at him on the gallops when he was back in training and were confronted with a fairly unprepossessing, light-framed bay that didn't set any of our pulses racing. And yet, by the time his first race for us came (in late August) he seemed to have filled out and muscled up and looked far more the part. So we went along to Market Rasen, a favourite course of mine, with excellent facilities for owners, hoping he would put in a good run but knowing he was going to get beaten. This would be the second of three completed novice hurdles required for the handicapper to give him a handicap mark. We knew that, inevitably, there were some very expensive, class animals in the field and that he wasn't going to get near them at level weights. As long as he beat a few and went well we would be quite happy. We would also be happy if he just came home safe and sound, it goes without saying. Snowy's breakdown in that last race was still on our minds.

Well, he did beat several home and the mission had been accomplished and about three and a half weeks later he ran again at the same course in a similar race and was then handed his handicap mark. In fact, in that race he finished eighth of twelve, which hardly sounds spectacular but he was not very far behind some really good horses and beat others that he shouldn't have done. The handicapper only thought he was worth a mark of 80 but, in a way, that was good news as we thought he could easily have been put on a mark of 86 or 88. A mark in the 80s is pretty modest, however, and we knew, whatever the precise figure, we had not got a superstar on our hands. I think we knew that anyway.

Once a horse has been allocated his handicap mark you can, of course, enter him in a handicap. Handicaps, where each horse carries a different weight according to their supposed ability, are designed to make racing exciting by giving everyone an equal chance. In theory if the handicapper has got it right (although it never works out like this) all the horses in a handicap should finish together in a kind of multiple dead heat. But handicapping is more of an art than a science, I think, and all horses have good days and bad days and days when they either love or loathe the going or the track or both. There are so many variables but the theory of an equal chance still holds and all the horses running in a handicap are up against horses of a similar sort of class and ability to themselves. The races are banded for, say, horses rated 0–100 or 0–110 and so on up the scale. Although it must be said that if a horse were actually rated zero surely it must be dead?

Anyway, Joe's time to take his chance in a handicap had come and we were now in mid-October 2014 and going to my local track of Uttoxeter. This time we went off 16 to 1 instead of 100 to 1 but he never did seem to show his best at Uttoxeter and he finished just an okay fifth of eleven, although he had not been beaten by all that much and had been doing his best work at the end of the race, moving through the field nicely.

Maybe he needed an extra half mile, John thought. So that was the next plan about a month later at Doncaster and everything seemed to be going smoothly and to plan until halfway along the back straight on the second circuit. Adrian Lane was riding that day and we knew immediately that something was amiss when he started to look down and pull him up. He had bled for the first time and quite badly. By a bleed I mean a nose bleed, which in human terms doesn't sound that bad, but it is something more serious in equine terms. Most racehorses bleed internally into the lungs, it is thought, at some point in their career due to the stress of galloping for two to three miles at a time. However, only in a comparative few horses does the bleed 'spill over' as it were, and start coming out of their nose. It is not a pretty sight to see and not at all pleasant for the poor horse. As soon as the bleed starts the horse will usually stop dead in its tracks, effectively pulling itself up. This is what happened to Joe down the back straight at Doncaster. At least we knew straight away what the problem was and that, thank God, it was not a 'leg' or other injury that would have meant a year or more off course. With a bleed, the horse just needs a short time to recover and a rest from racing for several weeks. The problem with 'bleeders', however, is that if they bleed once they're prone to bleed again and, if it occurs too frequently, it can be career-threatening. Anyway, chances were that this was a one off. Even some truly great horses have had the odd bleed. I remember that marvellous grey One Man – Hennessy Gold Cup winner, Queen Mother Champion Chase winner – bleeding a couple of times and stopping dead in his tracks. So, although it was a worry at the time, we knew Joe would come out of it and be able to race again fairly soon.

His recovery, I recall, was hampered somewhat by the fact that Joe, along with other horses in the stable, came down with a bit of a bug. John's horses were not quite right for a month or two around Christmas and they had to have the appropriate medication to clear up the problem – then there was the withdrawal time after they had taken the drugs. Such are the joys of owning a racehorse.

It was, therefore, February before Joe was healthy and fully fit to run again and his Doncaster run had been right at the end of November. Patience, again, is another great virtue for racehorse owners.

So, Sedgefield. It was in February, Joe's first run at the course he was eventually to love so much and his first visit there since being delivered there from Ireland. Steven Mulqueen was on board and, amazingly, he was backed down from 50 to 1 to 20 to 1 in places. Now, it so happened that our previous trainer's son, Tom Fife, was a course bookmaker and was standing at Sedgefield that day. He was a really nice chap and those of us there saw him on his plinth and said 'hello' and had a chat with him. We also had bets at 50 to 1 with him and he even said that, since he knew us, he'd give us an extra 10 per cent – hence we got odds of 55 to 1! Not bad, but then, he didn't think he would have to worry about paying us out. Fiddler's Flight, he thought, stood no chance.

We felt otherwise though. He had been going well at home. His Uttoxeter and Market Rasen form made him well-handicapped here and he was still quite unexposed. Anyway, some punters must have agreed because there was sufficient money put on him to bring his odds in considerably. And our faith in him was rewarded for the first time.

He was held up at the rear of the field but began to slide, almost unnoticed, through the field in a the home straight and, suddenly, to our joy, it was between him and one other horse going for the line. He seemed to have come from nowhere and Joe was still coming and coming but couldn't quite get to the other horse and he was beaten half a length in a thrilling finish. We were overjoyed. We were in the winner's enclosure with Joe for the first time, even if it was next to the 'second' sign. And we enjoyed collecting our winnings from Tom and being able to say 'we told you so'. We now knew we had a decent horse who could improve.

There then followed the biggest mistake I have made in my racehorse ownership 'career', if that is the correct word. It turned out to be a salutary experience which I have learned from and promised never to repeat. There was a good race for him back at

Sedgefield eighteen days later. A similar contest in fact over two miles and one furlong and, although he had been raised by the handicapper to the giddy heights of a mark of 84, we still all thought he was pretty well treated. It seemed just the right race for him and surely he wouldn't have the misfortune to be headed half a length again by an even better-handicapped horse. So that was the plan, except there was a problem that arose after we had entered him but before he was declared to run. If a jumps horse (it's slightly different these days) is entered to run on, say, a Wednesday, he will have to be entered by the trainer, online, the preceding Thursday. He will then be declared to run the day before the race which, in this example, would of course be the Tuesday. So there is a gap of several days between entry and declaration where things can go wrong or circumstances change. That is why if, say, there are thirty entries for a race, by the time declaration day comes along, usually only about half of that number will go to post. The horse could have had an injury or had not been working well at home or had been entered also for an alternative race elsewhere. In addition, things can drastically happen to the going in five days. Soft can become good, good can become heavy depending on the weather – and that was the problem.

We were experiencing a dry spell at the beginning of March 2015 and, whereas the going had been good to soft, soft in places for his previous run, this time, just before declaration day, they were giving it good, good to soft in places. Now John already said that he would only want to run him if the word 'soft' appeared somewhere in the going report. He thought that would be his favoured ground, plus there is less chance of injury to the horse's tendons on softer ground. John, touch wood, has a low percentage of lame horses for just that reason. He would never even consider running a horse on ground that said 'firm' in the going report.

John phoned me up, however, the day before Joe was due to be declared and said, 'I think we should put a pencil through this Sedgefield race, Phil. I know it says good, good to soft in places, but it's drying ground with no rain in the forecast and I know how crusty it can get at Sedgefield in these conditions.'

Now, I have always preached that the trainer should make all the decisions about running a horse, particularly a syndicate horse, and should not be swayed by the short-term desires of the owners. I would always argue that it is no good running a horse on unsuitable ground just because the owners fancy a nice day out at a particular course. But in this instance, I found myself going against my own edict. I really fancied Joe's chances in this race, especially on that course and against the opposition that would be lined up against him. It seemed too good an opportunity to be missed, especially as the end of the season was starting to loom. And, after all, it did mention 'soft' somewhere in the going report as I rationalised. John had said we could run if 'soft' was mentioned.

Sadly, as it turned out, John capitulated and agreed to run him and I am still beating myself up about my stupidity in putting pressure on John. It could have been a whole lot worse as there was no permanent damage done, but it was clear from the off that Joe was hating the ground and not moving as he should be. Then Stephen Mulqueen pulled him up going out onto the second circuit. He had bled again and it had been all my fault. Poor Joe, an anxious sort of horse at the best of times, had been worried about the going and, because of that anxiety, had had another nose bleed.

As I said, Joe was okay in the long run and, because the dry spell continued into the spring, it was the end of his season anyway. He went out into his field and I had learned my lesson. I swear I will never try and influence any trainer ever again in those sort of running decisions.

So it was the horse's summer holidays a bit earlier than planned due to his mishap and also the dry weather. It actually turned out to be a pretty long break for Joe. It was eight months almost exactly before he saw a racecourse again because the ground didn't start to really soften until the beginning of November. A long time off like that can, potentially, pose a problem if you're running a syndicate. It's just a thing to look out for if you are ever thinking of going down that route. Watch for unrest amongst the partners because, after all, they are paying the same monthly subscription but not getting to the races. Sometimes if they are not racing or 'horsey' people it may seem to them as if they are just living on promises. No such troubles for me now, however, although this sort of scenario had lost me the odd partner previously.

Our little brood, however, were well set by now and big supporters of both Joe and John. Maybe me as well, I hope.

One event I did plan, and we tend to do this every year now, was a meet-up at John's stables on a Saturday morning in early October when the horse was just starting his fast work and not far off a run. We would all go to High Hoyland and watch him do a piece of work (e.g., gallop) have a walk round and see his other horses and then sojourn to the pub for lunch. I can personally recommend the Cherry Tree in High Hoyland for good pub grub, decent ale and a friendly welcome, although it has recently changed hands and some reports have not been so good – so beware. Any other opportunity of getting the group together during the off season is also highly recommended and, during a couple of summers, John actually loaned us a horse of his own to run on the flat carrying our colours. Kingswinford one summer and most recently Magic Ship got us all to the races, even if it was for that rude four-letter word beginning with F – flat!

The start of The Fellowship of the Rose – Rose D'April

Rose D'April in affectionate mood

Rose D'April in the stable yard at Peter Beaumonts's not long before his planned first run

Bengal Boy after his Bangor win

Benny jumps the last at Bangor ridden by David O'Meara

Benny surrounded by Brandsby Racing members after his Bangor victory

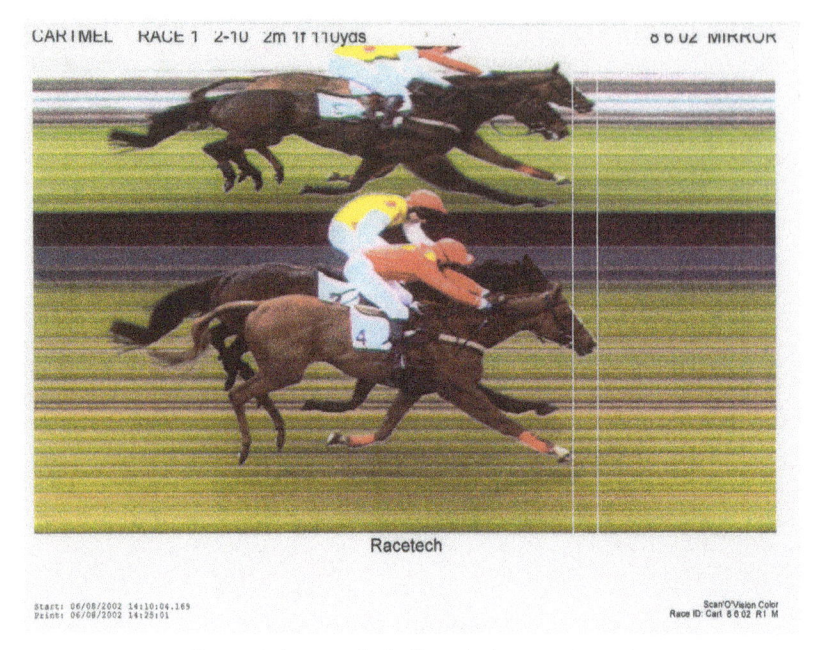

Benny is just touched off on the line at Cartmel

Stripe jumps the last to win at Bangor

Brandsby Stripe muddied in the winner's enclosure at Bangor

Stripe just gets his nose in front for his only win

Pinch Me Silver looking alert over the stable door

Pinch Me Silver in the parade ring ready for action

Just My Pal in action

Gaining Ground at Wetherby

Ritsi jumps the last at Wetherby and wins at a big price

Ritsi with mud spattered noseband after his win

Ritsi with adoring owners at the Wetherby presentation

Snow Alert goes to post under Stephen Mulqueen at Uttoxeter

Snow Alert takes a hurdle in good style at Uttoxeter

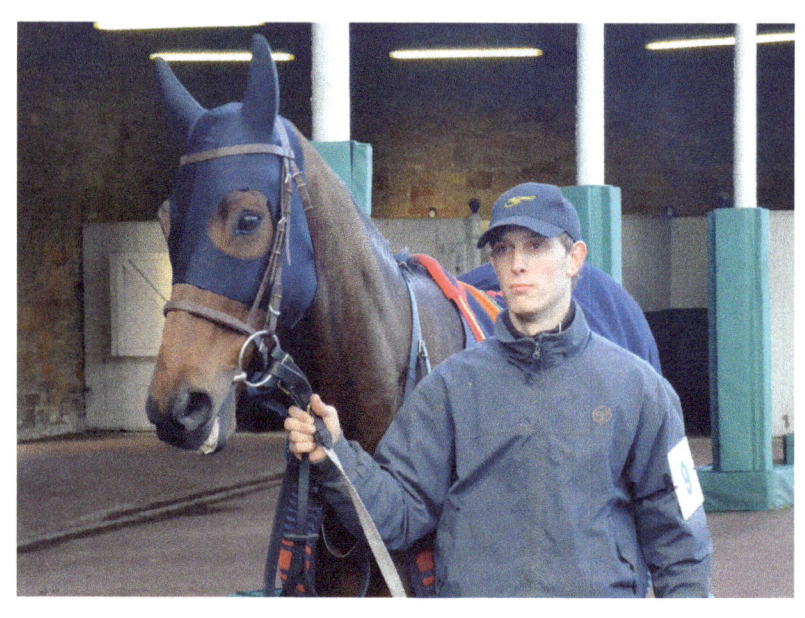

Joe in full head gear

Joe leaves the parade ring ready to go to post early

An after race de-briefing at Newcastle

Joe makes a blunder but still goes on to win at Sedgefield in the ride of the century

SEDGEFIELD
RACING & EVENTS
26th December 2015

Fiddler's Flight
Owner: Fellowship Of The Rose Partnership
Trainer: John Norton / Jockey: Colm McCormack
The Ministers Indian Restaurant Sedgefield Handicap Hurdle Race

Joe and Colm McCormack, both covered in mud, approach the winning post on their Sedgefield Boxing Day win

Colm stays on board somehow but seems to have thrown away his chance

The stirrupless Colm McCormack completes his famous victory at Sedgefield

Colm receives his ride of the year award

Happy connections at the presentations after Fiddlers Flight's second and most memorable win at Sedgefield

YESTERDAY AT THE RACES
TALK OF THE TRACKS

McCormack saves the day with fine recovery

Sedgefield
Colin Russell

WHO needs stirrup irons? Not claimer Colm McCormack, for in an incident similar to the one in which Ruby Walsh won on Killultagh Vic at Leopardstown last month he got Fiddler's Flight up to win the 2m1f handicap hurdle despite having neither foot in the irons.

Behind for much of the race, Fiddler's Flight was making ground on the two horses in front of him when he made a mistake at the last and went left.

Despite making a fine recovery, McCormack's right foot came out of the iron and his saddle slipped round a little. However, by kicking his other foot free he got his mount up in the last couple of strides to win by half a length.

After his fourth winner of the season the winning rider said: "He can be a bit of a sketchy jumper so I wanted just to pop the last but he got it wrong, nearly got me off and his saddle went. I'd lost one iron so I kicked the other one out and he got there."

The winner is trained by John Norton, who said: "That was a brilliant ride. It shows what a good jockey Colm is, I'm surprised he doesn't get a lot more rides."

George bounces back
Retirement has been put on hold for My Friend George, who made it three wins from four runs on the course with a game success in the 2m5f handicap chase.

Well beaten at Ayr on his previous start having been put up 8lb for his win here on Boxing Day, he bounced back in fine style, coming from off the pace under Henry Brooke to beat the favourite Verko by six lengths.

He is owned by Arthur Slack and trained by his son Ken, who said: "We were thinking about retiring him but we'll keep him going now."

Colm McCormack: just got up

Racing Post headlines after Colm's 'ride of the century'

Yours truly on horseback in dressage mode – sort of

And then about to disappear down the hay field

Jockey Colm McCormack in our racing colours

Sedgefield

The start of Joe's new season, however, did begin to dawn eventually. November came around, the ground had eased and he was duly entered for a two-mile handicap hurdle at Uttoxeter – a popular choice – to kick off his 2015 campaign. It was to prove to be his, and our, most memorable one ever.

A new jockey for him as well. I had vaguely heard the name Colm McCormack before, but John had been giving him a few rides during the summer and was impressed by the way he rode, plus the fact they got on well together. Colm proved to be a real horseman, not just a jockey, and he was the one who found the key to Joe as they formed a really effective partnership.

I remember I had gone that day to Uttoxeter minus my usual headgear. No trilby, no flat cap. I don't know how I managed to forget a hat since the forecast was for heavy rain during the afternoon. The forecast was spot on so I was forced to part with £20 or thereabouts, on an emergency replacement cap which luckily someone was selling from a stall at the racecourse. The weather was filthy with constant heavy rain from about midday onwards and the going (always a bit on the soft side at Uttoxeter in winter) soon became heavy. No problem about the going being too lively for him this time then, but, on the other hand, he had never experienced going quite as deep as this before.

We need not have worried as Colm settled him in near the rear and let him lob along at his own pace. This was the key I referred to before. Joe did not like to be hassled and hustled or pushed and shoved along to keep up. If he could settle into his own, comfortable stride for the first half of the race and ignore the other horses around him, he was fine. He didn't feel stressed or out of his comfort zone. Hence, no nose bleeds. John had also decided to put a hood on him which covered his ears. We had noticed how excited and anxious he became before the start of the race when he heard the sounds of the crowd. The hood cut out that noise for him. At some point, also, I think it may have been at his first Sedgefield race, John asked the stewards if he could go down to the start early before the other horses. It is a request that is usually granted and that certainly made a difference too. Instead of him getting wrought up and sweating at the start he seemed to settle down much better. Because he was going to post early it also meant that he only had to be led around the parade ring once, maybe twice, before the jockey mounted. Then he was out and off down to the start – again without time to get himself anxious. What a delicate flower he was but all this special treatment was to pay off.

Back at Uttoxeter, after he had settled nicely at the rear of the field, Colm began to ask him to slice his way through the field, which he was doing really well. Enough to start to give us a bit of excitement. He came through from his last place to finish a decent sixth of thirteen and it looked as if he still had plenty of running left in him at the end.

The only criticism of Colm's riding that anyone made was that perhaps he had left him too much to do and should have ridden him a little closer to the pace from the off. But Colm stuck to his guns and was convinced he had found the best way to ride Joe. He was right, of course, because he was the horseman and we were just worried owners. My advice is, always let the professionals get on and do their job and keep your comments to yourself. We all went away from Uttoxeter drenched but feeling a lot better about Joe. No bleed. He had settled well and we all felt there was better to come.

Next stop was Newcastle, about three weeks later in a similar race. A long way to go but Colin (co-owner and 'acolyte') drove me there and back along with a friend of mine who also fancied a day out at Newcastle races and who took some good photographs of the day's proceedings, by the way.

The weather that winter continued to be appallingly wet. It had hardly stopped raining since the Uttoxeter meeting and, although on the day of the Newcastle meeting, the sun was out and it was a glorious, crisp early December day, the ground there was heavy. Officially it was 'heavy, soft in places' but I don't know where they managed to find any soft places. It all seemed pretty bottomless to me.

The plan was the same again. Colm was going to drop him in at the back of the field and let him go at his own, happy pace. And the outcome was similar to his last race. He unleashed him down the home straight where he came from last to fifth this time, but closer to the winner and probably unfortunate not to get a place.

I remember clearly afterwards Colm's words. 'Don't worry,' he said, 'one day all the horses in front of him will collapse in a heap on going like this and he'll win for you.' Prophetic words. It was now Christmas 2015 and John had given him an entry at Sedgefield for Boxing Day. John thought it would be a popular decision to give everyone a chance of a day's racing in the holiday season. The strange thing was, though, that all except me had other family commitments on Boxing Day and so, ironically, couldn't make it. I, however, had no such commitments and, after having our Christmas Day dinner, was all geared up for the trip north. December had still continued to be wet pretty well all over the country. It rained, rained, rained. A lot of the traditional Boxing Day fixtures were under threat from the weather. Sedgefield's going, hardly surprisingly, was heavy and on Christmas Day evening I searched the internet and on Twitter for any news of an abandonment. Wetherby had already been called off and, with more rain forecast, particularly for the north of England, I was half convinced that our meeting would go the same way. No news that night though, and when I awoke in the morning we had had no more rain overnight in Derbyshire, so things were hopeful. Then on BBC News they were telling us all about torrential rain all night and floods in the north. Even worse, the rain was set to continue up there all day. It was back to checking the Sedgefield website and their Twitter feed for news of, I thought, an almost inevitable abandonment.

But the meeting was still being given as on and I had to leave early as it was a two-and-a-half-hour drive and an early start to the meeting, it being now midwinter.

On Radio 5 Live the sports bulletin was giving out plenty of race meetings and football matches abandoned because of the rain but Sedgefield it confidently said, was still on. So, still more in hope than expectation, I set off at shortly after 8 a.m. for County Durham. The weather was dry as far as Doncaster or thereabouts and then I ran into rain and it looked as if they had already had plenty deposited there. Driving north on the A1 I kept tuning in at regular intervals to the sports bulletins to listen out for any news of, I thought, the inevitable abandonment. But no, Sedgefield was still going ahead.

When I got as far as Wetherby I was already aware, of course, that the meeting there had been called off, but I wasn't expecting to see a lake where usually there is a racecourse by the side of the motorway. All there was to be seen on both sides of the road was water. In the distance the stands were still visible above the water line, but the jumps, the rails and everything else were submerged! How on earth could Sedgefield still be on? But it was given out on every bulletin that racing would go ahead.

It was very, very soggy at Sedgefield. That is a gross understatement. And, what is more, it was still raining. Maybe it wasn't a torrent anymore but it was steady. We were in the sixth race of a seven race card and it did occur to me that, even if racing did get underway, the meeting could still be abandoned halfway through if the rain persisted. I began to wonder what on earth I was doing there. I just hoped it would all be worth it.

'There's only you and me here today, John,' I remember saying to the trainer when we met up in the owners and trainers.

'Yes,' he replied. 'We're the only two stupid enough to be here.' Full of the same doubts that I had about the viability of the meeting going ahead.

The first five races came and went and I had enjoyed a plateful of the hearty food that they serve up for the owners and trainers at Sedgefield. And still the rain continued to fall. There was now news filtering through of whole areas of Sheffield and Rochdale and Huddersfield, and God knows where else, being flooded out and homes forsaken. Yet still we were racing.

Then, after the fifth race, the stewards called for a group of senior jockeys and trainers to walk the course to assess whether it was still raceable. I feared the worst and it was very much in the balance. The result of the inspection came back and was announced. They said, to a man and a woman, that it was still raceable and that the last two races were definitely going ahead as planned.

So we were, amazingly, still in business and off went John to get the horse saddled up and ready for the, now usual, procedure. Colm rode him once round the parade ring and then went down to the start early. He had told me that the plan was to drop him in at the rear, as was becoming customary, not to hassle him and then hope to pick them off one by one. The rain persisted and all the horses eventually splashed off through the wet and the mud to join Joe at the start.

John and I decided the best view of the race would probably be just by the bookies' enclosure next to the parade ring on some raised steps. Visibility was not great but from there we had a good view of the big screen as well as the course. Soon we were underway, Joe being, dutifully, dropped in at the rear. You could clearly see as they approached the stands on the first circuit the puddles that had now formed on the track. They splashed through them, mud flying everywhere. It was a sight I had never seen on a racecourse before or since, but, nevertheless, the conditions didn't seem to inconvenience them too much. I think it was so soft that they just sluiced straight through it. That mud was beyond holding them down, it was now liquid.

Joe was out the back as planned and going into the second circuit was in last place. That was okay. He was still in the race and plenty of distance to go. Going out onto the back straight he was still in last place, but were we bothered? No! This was still the plan and anyway, who dared to think about him going on to win or anything as ridiculous as that? At least he was still there with some sort of a chance of picking us up a bit of prize money.

They turned into the home straight with just a few hurdles left to jump and at that point he began to pass a couple and then a couple more. He was moving into a position where he might be able to put in a challenge. My word! Then, with two to jump he was suddenly right up there with the leaders. He popped the second last well and all of a sudden, coming to the final obstacle, he was looking like the winner. John and I as we stood next to each other looked at one another and we could see each of us was thinking 'Crikey this could be it!' He came to the last just having to get over, but crashed straight through it. Oh no. Was he going to come down? No, not quite. He picked himself up somehow. He hardly seemed to be slowed down or inconvenienced at all by his awful blunder in fact. He got himself going again straight away and scooted up the Sedgefield hill and hit the winning post – first!

That was the first and, at the time of writing, the only occasion I have been hugged by the trainer. His joy was as unbounded as mine. Joe, Fiddler's Flight, had just won a race for us. Our awkward, untrainable, quirky horse had just finished in first place for us all in a horse race. Never mind that it was at Sedgefield and not at Kempton on Boxing Day. That didn't matter one tiny bit. He had done it for us and – wow – at that precise moment in time nothing felt better in the world.

We welcomed the horse and Colm back to the winner's enclosure and then I was presented with a memento by the owners of the local Indian restaurant that had sponsored the race. They even invited me for a free meal at their restaurant that evening but I had to make my excuses because I still had to drive 150 miles southward that night back to Derbyshire despite a glass of celebratory champagne.

Every time I rerun that race, even now, I think 'How on earth did the meeting go ahead and, also, how on earth did he hit that last hurdle so hard and not be affected by it?' Whatever – we had won. Joe, God bless him, was a winner.

My only reservation was that I was there on my own as an owner. That is not withstanding the trainer's hug. However, everyone else had been watching the race one way or another and phone calls and texts of course began to come pouring in. What a Christmas present that had been, and the next thing was, as always with racing folk, to look forward to his next run.

It came a month later, in January, at Catterick, a flatter course and, perhaps, not perfect for him, but he was an 8 to 1 chance with every hope. In this race, however, it became obvious that he was never quite going to get there and, in any case, just as he had been moving through smoothly as before, he came to the second last and – oops – he unseated Colm as he hit the hurdle pretty hard.

Colm afterwards, nursing a bruised backside suffered by a kick from another horse's hoof as he tumbled, said he thought he would have finished third if he had stayed on. We thought fourth might have been more realistic, but still, it was not a bad run.

The only downside to appear was the fact that, after he had returned to the stables, he was seen to bleed a little again from his nose. It was nothing severe at all but it had to be reported. I think it was the stress of losing his jockey that triggered it off. I honestly think he looked up and thought, 'Oh no, my rider's disappeared. What do I do now?' I'm convinced that the pressure of that unexpected situation brought on his slight bleed.

Joe survived though and was basically okay after his race. The good thing now was that he was becoming consistent and we were getting a bit used to the idea that, whenever he ran, he might just stand a chance of winning and that was a new experience. His odds were always in single figures and we weren't there just to make up the numbers anymore.

After that Catterick run there was a plan to race him back at Sedgefield again a couple of weeks later. Sedgefield certainly seemed to suit him and so he was entered for a two-mile handicap on 9 February 2016. That proved to be a highly significant date and it is a date forever etched on my memory. I still occasionally go back to that date on the At The Races Replays website and have a quick look, if only at the end part of the race. But more of that later.

On 9 February there was, I'm pleased to say, an excellent turnout of the members of our syndicate. A full house, as I remember, plus Colin's wife too as they just happened to be on a short trip up in that part of the world anyway. A visit to the Northumberland coast, I think. It is great when there is a good group of you there, much better than when I was on my own on Boxing Day, as great as that experience was.

I think, in fact, the main argument in favour of small syndicates is that, apart from, obviously, spreading the cost of racing, it makes for a potentially memorable shared experience that can be jointly recalled over and over again at subsequent meetings. There were just seven runners in his race with Colm up as normal and he was sent off at 8 to 1 which, I think, was pretty generous. He had his favourite going – soft, heavy in places and, as normal again, he went through his usual routine of being led just once round the parade ring and then down to the start early to let him settle. Then, the nerves in our stomachs just before the off, followed by the race unfolding. And just how it did unfold!

The plan, of course, all along was to drop Joe in behind and let him go along at his comfortable pace. It had worked a dream on Boxing Day and Colm, being tuned into the horse by now, knew exactly what was right for him. We were used to him being in the rear. That was okay. But, going along the back straight on the second circuit he was still so far out the rear that we were seriously beginning to think something was amiss with him. John and I had parted from the main group and we were based in our customary spot by the side of the betting ring. I could just not work out what was going on as the course commentator kept calling, 'And way out the back, detached from the rest is Fiddler's Flight.'

Approaching the bend at the end of the back straight I recall turning to John and saying something like, 'I know the plan was to drop him in at the back, but is this still the plan?'

'No, Phil, no. This is not the plan. I don't know what's going on. All I can say is that if he wins from here it'll be a miracle.' That was his gloomy reply.

Then, turning into the home straight, our ears did prick up a little when the commentator said that Fiddler's Flight was picking up a bit and had managed to pass a couple of tired horses. Then into the straight for the last time with a line of three hurdles to face. Suddenly, more horses were beginning to struggle in front of him and, as if from nowhere, two out he had come right through the entire field to dispute third place. How could it have happened? I turned to John between that flight and the last and said, 'My God. We're going to get third here. Fantastic.'

But then, approaching the last, the commentator was saying, 'Just look at Fiddler's Flight, who was some way off the pace earlier in the race, coming through.'

Joe got to the last and, amazingly, I realised that all he had to do was to pop it and he was the winner. He was going so much better than all the others and there were only two other horses by this time with even the remotest chance. The others were either all well behind or had been pulled up. He got to that last hurdle and – oh no – I could not believe it. He blundered exactly as he had done on Boxing Day, only this time a whole lot worse. Not only did his mistake slow him right down this time, but it also nearly jettisoned Colm out of the saddle. It looked as if he would disappear out of the side door but somehow he managed to scramble back into the saddle. By now, though he had lost seven or eight lengths on the other two horses and, we noticed, was also riding without irons. He had lost one at the hurdle and had decided to kick the other one free and so rode that final furlong minus stirrups, his legs dangling long like some old time 19th century jockey. It was rodeo stuff.

'Now Colm McCormack has lost his irons. That's not going to help his cause,' bellowed the commentator. It certainly wasn't but good old Joe just put his head down and went for the line. Suddenly, against all known odds, he came through on a wet sail and passed the two leaders.

'And here comes Fiddler's Flight,' went the commentary. 'He's getting there. Fiddler's Flight and Colm McCormack. A fantastic ride.'

John turned to me and said, 'Have we won?' and I said, 'Yes of course we've won. God knows how but we've won.'

The ecstasy on everyone's faces when we met up straight afterwards must have been a sight to behold. This was a win but it was not just an ordinary win. We knew that immediately. This was a win that not just we as owners, but lots and lots of other racing fans were going to remember and talk about for ages. And it was our humble, somewhat quirky but incredibly brave and determined horse, Joe, that had done it.

It is totally impossible to put down in words what everyone was feeling at that point on that day at Sedgefield. All I can say is that it is moments like that which is what racehorse ownership is all about. It is why we do it and it is why anyone with the slightest inkling to get involved should do it. Not that you can ever guarantee precious, special moments like that, but you never know.

Well, of course, there were the post-race presentations and an interview with At The Races, where I remember Mick Fitzgerald saying, 'That's not just going to be the ride of the month or ride of the season. That's going to be the ride of the century.' We were only sixteen years and a bit into the century but he was definitely right.

At The Races do, of course, run a 'ride of the month' competition voted on by their viewers. A short list is drawn up and replayed for a number of days for people to make their selection. They then run a similar competition for 'ride of the year' where the 12 monthly winning rides are voted on by the public.

So what Mick Fitzgerald was saying was that Colm's ride on Joe was in his opinion the nailed on winner of not just the former prize but the latter one as well.

It turned out he was dead right. He swept the board on both counts and all without us having to twist the arms of as many friends and neighbours as we could think of to vote for him. There really was only one in it. And the recording of it is still there on At The Races Replays for all to see – over and over again if you want to. You just have to scroll all the way back to February 9th 2016 and click on Sedgefield, the last race of the day.

At the end of the year there was a black tie/evening dress presentation evening held where Colm was presented with a trophy for his ride of the year and, perhaps of more practical importance for him, a big fuel voucher worth into the thousands of pounds which would keep him on the road for a good while.

Tickets were limited which meant I could not go but Colm, his partner Hayley, his parents who came over from Ireland and

John Norton all went along. The winners were not announced until the night and, although we knew Colm was the favourite, it was still a bit tense waiting for the formal announcement. John said he would be on the phone to me as soon as they declared the victor but I managed to pre-empt him slightly by getting the result on Twitter and let out a silent cheer at home for Colm and Joe.

John, jokingly, said he should have got some credit too because if he had schooled the horse better Colm would never have won! That was one way of looking at it.

Meanwhile back on the day at Sedgefield I had all sorts of messages all of a sudden on my phone. I had to phone up Liz and tell her I might be a bit later home than planned because he had won again, but it was not as simple as that. It had been an extraordinary race and I would have to explain it all to her somehow when, eventually, I did return home.

The after-race celebrations are still something of a blur to be honest, but they kept on playing reruns of the finish as if to prove to people it had really happened. The whole race including the final outcome is not something anyone could ever have predicted. The most telling thing I do remember is Colin saying to me, as we were departing to the car parks at the end of the racing, that this had been, without a shadow of any doubt, the greatest day in racing he had ever experienced. This was from a guy who had had a runner with Nigel Twiston-Davies at Grade 1 level and had been around racing a long time and had visited nearly every racecourse in the Kingdom. Wow. What a compliment. It is still impossible to imagine how that day in February 2016 could possibly be bettered or even equalled.

The dust of that marvellous day settled eventually, but not until I had bought my copy of the Racing Post the next day to read the write-up and bask in our fifteen minutes, if I can call it that, of fame.

Well, those heady days with Joe were never recaptured and hardly surprisingly. How could that be surpassed? In his next race he finished a good third and the race after that he was fourth, again giving a good account of himself. He had developed into a very consistent performer. Then, in his last race of the season before the ground turned to 'good', at Bangor, he was only beaten by one horse on whom there had been a huge gamble that morning. It was almost a moral victory for Joe and the nearest thing there is these days to a 'fix'. Although, please let me assure everyone, particularly those who are not horse racing aficionados, that there can never be a real 'fix' anymore.

First, jockeys don't get together in the weighing room before the race and decide which of them is going to win. It is an impossibility and yet some stupid punters still seem to think that this sort of thing goes on. Second, you are never quite sure how a horse is going to run even if you have engineered it into a position where it should easily win off its current handicap mark. Whatever the case, Joe was beaten into second place that day by a horse that had clearly been laid out to win the race and gambled on accordingly. Afterwards its handicap mark was raised by about 20 pounds, we noticed. Our horse had run another great race though and we had all had another fantastic day out at the races with a runner who had done us proud. The only downside I can think of was the fact that the heavy going was not just restricted to the course but also to the car park. I, unfortunately, ended up being towed out of the Owners and Trainers car park at the end of the day's racing which proved frustrating, but I can honestly say that the Bangor-on-Dee tractor driver was excellent.

And that was the end of our 2015/16 season. A memorable one to say the least and still the most memorable we have ever had. Could there ever be a repeat of the emotions felt during that Sedgefield race of the century? I very much doubt it but we all hope there might be.

The very nature of racing is that you are always looking forward and tend to forget about the past, particularly if your horse has run a bad race. The next race is all that is important. After a summer out at grass in South Yorkshire, Joe was got up again for another assault on Britain's racecourses. Eventually, John got him out again on 2 November because, although the horse had been fit enough to run earlier, we had to wait for the ground to ease. We got the deluge, finally, that we required and it was soft/heavy in places at Sedgefield where he finished third to an old adversary of Joe's called Discoverie. Our new season was underway and we were, I guess, still full of expectations.

Sadly, Joe never quite recovered his form of the previous season although he was still giving his absolute all in his races. He did give us another four places during that season, notably when running second to an oddly-named horse called Frightened Rabbit, believe it or not, at Newcastle. That horse had practically bolted out of control for much of the race and held a lead still of probably 40 lengths coming into the straight. He had shot his bolt at the end and Joe finishing strongly as always, just failed to get to him and was beaten by a length. Joe's appetite for the game still seemed to be there and he still loved galloping around Sedgefield. We had never expected his exploits of the previous season to be surpassed or even equalled so we all had enjoyed going to the races again and see him give his best and battle through the usually atrocious conditions.

He was still an eleven-year old when the next season started and John kept saying, 'He didn't start till he was seven and there's no reason why he can't keep going until he's twelve or even older.'

That made eminent logic but, unfortunately, that year time did catch up on him. He did run a blindingly good race at Christmas to finish a very close third at a big price at Sedgefield, naturally. But that apart, his form began to tail off.

In three more races at his beloved Sedgefield he failed to get competitive plus one race at Wetherby and even a National Hunt flat race at Southwell! He was, hardly surprisingly, tailed off there but he was given the run because all the other meetings had been abandoned because of frost and snow. Do you remember the 'Beast from the East?'

The final nail was hammered in on 23 March 2018 at Sedgefield where he finally (and for the only time ever) threw in the towel on his favourite soft ground over two and a half miles. He just let us know he had enough of the game and Colm pulled him up. As John and I watched him from the stands we looked at each other and immediately knew what we were both thinking. Eventually, we had said previously, he would tell us when he was ready to retire and this run told us just that.

So that day marked the end of an era for us and there would be no more cheering on Joe. We could now only remember and cherish all his noble efforts for us. Joe was retired and went to a home, ironically, near Sedgefield in County Durham to be retrained as a riding horse and show jumper in local shows. He certainly deserved and had earned a happy and long retirement. And it did really feel like an end of an era.

The Junior Man

Joe left a big hole in our racing lives. But we still did have 'The Junior Man', who we had acquired in the previous autumn. He had already provided us with a bit of anticipatory interest during his novice hurdling season.

Now, I have not mentioned The Junior Man before, so I should really give you his background story now. During the previous summer I had done some sums and counted up my income and also did some calculations around the fact that we (Liz and I) intended to sell up our smallholding and downsize. We felt that we were now on our last two horses at home and wanted to have more time and flexibility to take holidays and more freedom from mucking out stables at 5:45 every morning. We knew that Joe was not getting any younger and perhaps I should look at the future, racing-wise. I worked out that, if John was willing to take a 50 per cent share of the horse, I could run the other half with or without the support of my fellow partners. I was hesitant, though, since we hadn't actually sold our property yet (which would have put a considerable amount of money in our bank account), but Liz supported my idea and told me to 'go for it', if that was what I really wanted.

It just so happened that in the spring of that year I had gone with John to the Goff's Doncaster sales just for the sheer experience of it. I had been there once before when at Peter's on the day he bought Hussard Collonges, his future RSA Chase winner at the Cheltenham Festival, but that was many years earlier. The sales are absolutely fascinating and I wholeheartedly recommend anyone interested in racing to make a trip there and make a day out of it, if only once in their lives. To see the bidding go up and up and up for a really beautiful horse, into six figures, and to see the auctioneer bouncing bids back and forth between the two bidders on opposite sides of the hall until the hammer finally falls is electrifying.

I digress here slightly, though, because John's bidding limit was quite a bit lower. He was there because he wanted to purchase a National Hunt horse at a reasonable price to put in 'his shop window' as he calls it. A horse, in other words, that he can sell on to a potential owner who may contact him to see if he has anything available in the yard.

'If you've got nothing in the shop window, you can't sell owt,' said John.

On that day as I followed him around the boxes looking at different horses, he kept coming back to a nice-looking bright bay called The Junior Man. He was four and had raced in three point-to-points in Ireland. On his last race he had finished third of, I think, five but had not been beaten by very much. He certainly did catch the eye as a good-looking horse and was well put together. During the day we kept looking at him and had him trotted up for us as you would. I liked him, John liked him too and he would be within his price range too. In the end he made about £5,000 and became the property of J R Norton Limited.

John initially thought he had a ready purchaser for his new acquisition but they were time wasters and it all fell through. It was at this point, in the late summer, that I approached John about The Junior Man and put forward the proposition of buying him. He was still available and John thought he might make a half-decent National Hunt horse and, if I wanted him, he was mine. I must have referred back to my other half, who was still very supportive, and a purchase price was worked out. Junior, as he was known in the stable, became mine and I must have obviously mentioned this to my other syndicate members. As it turned out, and to my surprise, all of them said something like, 'He sounds a really nice horse and I'd like a share in him.' Maybe it was my natural sales ability or something but I really wasn't desperate for the others to join in. In fact, I would have been more than happy to have had a horse on my own, but I just couldn't shake them off! That's an indication of just how close a little group of like spirits we had become.

So Junior became a Fellowship of the Rose horse and was put into full training for us, it turned out, as a successor to the wonderful Joe, but their careers overlapped by a season, i.e., Junior's novice hurdle season.

But Junior was never, sadly, to make the grade as a racehorse. He was never quite tough enough mentally as much as physically, which is always an important factor to take into consideration. Junior had always some ability, as much as and maybe more than Joe's, but he turned out to be a repeated 'bleeder'. Joe, you will recall, bled occasionally when he came under extreme stress, as he would have seen it, but Junior, in the end, was having a nose bleed every time he raced. Eventually, just under a year after Joe's final race, we decided to retire Junior from the track at the age of only seven. Once again he had told us that at Sedgefield. He had to be pulled up by Colm on the back straight on the last circuit and, when he came back to the enclosures, the poor lad's nose was pumping out blood. It was a sad and sorry sight and you just could not have kept subjecting him to that. He was so distressed and it was awful to see him in that condition.

We had been very patient with him and tried to give him every chance. He was, also, a beautifully put together horse. He was very handsome and always looked the part. He looked as though one day he would make a half-decent chaser, but it was never to be and, thankfully, again he was really well-homed.

John found an excellent new home for him. We sold him for what was under his possible market price for such a stamp of horse. He went to a mother and daughter team who lived quite locally near Barnsley. Initially he would be kept at livery but, in the longer term he was to go with the daughter, who was eighteen, to college in York. She was going to take an equestrian course there. He was much loved and cherished and soon was plastered all over Facebook because she loved him to bits. What a happy ending for the horse and, in a way, for us as well, because it feels so good that a horse who has given everything he can for you is going to be looked after and loved, we hope, for the rest of his life.

Perhaps this is a good opportunity to take a little time out to talk about the aftercare of racehorses when they leave the track. It has become a topic very close to my heart and, in a way, I think I am playing a minor part in their cause.

The British Thoroughbred Retraining Centre

In the summer of 2017 I noticed in the newsletter that I routinely received from the British Thoroughbred Retraining Centre that they were looking for people to offer themselves as possible trustees for the charity. I knew that the charity existed to retrain ex-racehorses for a life after racing in equestrian disciplines but other than that I knew very little about it. I think I received the newsletter because of my involvement with horseracing and I did know that the organisation had been formed some years earlier by a person called Carrie Humble. We had even gone up to their then headquarters to have a look around back in the '90s to see what work they were doing and came back impressed. But I wasn't very well informed about the current work of the charity.

I decided, anyway, to send a letter of application, encouraged by Liz, because it sounded to be an organisation I really believed in. I thought I would probably not hear anything more – an acknowledgement maybe at the most. However, eventually I did receive a reply and, to my astonishment, they were inviting me for an interview. If nothing else, that in itself was quite flattering, so I made my way up the M6 to the BTRC in North Lancashire. It was late summer 2017 and the traffic on the motorway was desperate thanks to road works, but eventually I arrived there with a few minutes to spare to find a wonderfully positioned and excellently equipped equine facility with views across the North Pennines.

I met the chairman of the charity, John Sexton (who is a former Racing Post journalist), his CEO Gillian Carlisle and one of the existing board members, Michelle Metz. The interview turned out to be less like an interview and more like a conversation between like-minded people. We all obviously did believe deeply in racehorses having the chance of a good life after racing. I always felt particularly sorry for those poor, small flat racers who had failed on the course and who form the bulk of the BTRC's re-trainees. Older horses who have learned how to jump an obstacle are easier to re-home. However, youngsters whose only education has been to gallop flat out in a straight line are more problematical.

We must have covered every aspect of life for racehorses after racing but I remember being especially grilled about my attitude to euthanasia.

The BTRC policy is that, given the fact that a large proportion of their referrals are welfare cases, if horses that can never be successfully retrained for any other discipline because of physical (or sometimes mental) problems, they have to be, sadly, put to sleep. I, of course, knew that this has to be the best policy. Eventually all of us who own any animal, great or small, will have to make this decision and judge when it is the 'right thing' to do and also when it is the right time to do it. I remember a wise vet once saying that it is always better to put down an animal a week too soon than a week too late.

Apparently some people are either two sentimental or too squeamish to accept that sometimes it is better for the horse to be put down than live out its days, half-crippled and semi-neglected in some small, muddy paddock.

I had no such qualms and that seemed to be very important to my interviewers.

Eventually, after having had a tour of the stables and other facilities I went away from the BTRC very impressed with the work they were doing and their dedication to serving the best interests of the thoroughbred horse.

They told me that they had plenty more people to interview and that they would be in touch shortly, but it was the first interview I had ever attended where it really didn't matter to me what the outcome would be. In previous interviews, when I was keen to get the job, it could have made huge differences to my income, location, workload and much more, but in this instance, I was merely interested in offering, for free, whatever little expertise I may be able to offer.

Several weeks elapsed, in fact, before I had any response. I thought that, almost certainly, I had been forgotten, but then, unexpectedly, I received a letter from the Northwest.

It was rather strangely worded, because at first it sounded as if it was going to be a let-down letter.

'We had a very large response', 'it was very difficult to choose' etc. But then it went on to say they were delighted to offer me the position as a trustee of the BTRC. I was simultaneously surprised and delighted and I am still very proud to hold that position and to have seen things progress, in only a few years, so far in terms of the aftercare of racehorses. It has certainly become much higher in the perception of the general public and, perhaps more importantly, in a perception of the horseracing authorities. Aftercare should never be just a PR exercise, however. It should be a real, hands on reality. But, nevertheless, PR is also important and now I think the BHA realises just that.

The BTRC is a charity that does amazing work and is the largest centre of its kind in the country with a huge amount of experience at its disposal and has just celebrated its thirtieth birthday. It was founded by Carrie Humble in 1991 and from small, humble (pardon the pun) beginnings has flourished to become a real centre of excellence and, most importantly, it has helped an awful lot of retired racehorses have a better life. It has become easily the largest retraining centre in the land and at least I have played a very small part in that. It should be pointed out anyway that the vast proportion of racehorses find excellent retirement homes or, at least, homes where they can perform other equine sports. Most trainers are caring enough these days, to find them such homes and most will not have to even consider a retraining facility. But the BTRC (and the other similar, if smaller, centres) provide an essential and vital safety net.

Black Market

Well, after Junior, we thought that might be the end of the road. After all, we had had our fifteen minutes of fame with Joe and maybe by now everyone had run out of either money or will or both. But no. Always in racing there is tomorrow and somehow real enthusiasts manage to scrape sufficient bits of money together. So it was decided, after a meeting of the syndicate members in a pub in Uttoxeter, to go off to Doncaster sales in August to see if we could get a cheap (up to £18,000 was our budget – so not that cheap) successor to Junior. Actually, come to think of it, £18,000 is very cheap compared to the top price paid on the day of £280,000, but you could still get a half-decent horse or better within our price range.

So the search had to be started and once the catalogue had plopped through my letterbox, I commenced scouring that publication for a likely and realistic replacement.

A lot of horses on offer from Ireland had already run, often as just four-year-olds, in Irish point-to-points. These races are slightly different to what most people regard as point-to-points in this country. In Britain, they are races for horses, usually a lot older than four, that have been hunted that season with a particular hunt. The riders are all amateur and the horses are mainly of inferior ability to those running in professional National Hunt racing. They are, on the whole, a version of steeplechasing for people involved and participating in hunting who have a thoroughbred they think will be able to do the job of racing whilst giving them a bit of fun and excitement. They are certainly not for the faint-hearted and the standard of both horses and riders seems to be improving, but they are not like Irish points.

The Irish version is largely aimed at the breeders of young thoroughbreds who want to sell their youngsters at a good price at auction. They provide a shop window, if you like, for those breeders to sell their wares. If you have a five- or maybe a four-year-old who can gallop and jump, you enter it into one of these points. I'm not quite sure how you qualify them to run in these races. In Britain, the horse has to have been certified as going out hunting on so many days with a recognised hunt before it can race in a point. It may be more lax in Ireland, given that the purpose of the races is different.

An Irish point is usually run over three miles but it can be less because, as I say, four-year-olds frequently take part and you might not want to run a horse that young over too long a distance. Okay, the jumps are pretty easy, but the going can be quite a test (across farmers' fields that may not have been brilliantly rolled, for instance). But a convincing winner of such a contest can easily make £40,000 to £50,000 at Doncaster if they have been sufficiently impressive. In fact you can even double or treble those figures for the most outstanding specimens.

I probably will not go down the route of Irish point-to-point form again, but at the time I thought it was probably the best route for us, as did John. So I spent days and days studying form and watching any available video of the races that had been put on line.

At the end of the process John and I had drawn up a shortlist between us and off we went to Goff's sales at Doncaster full of hope and expectation.

Well, our prime target we just missed out on. It went for £2,000 more than our absolute top budget price and other horses we had fancied on paper turned out to be disappointments on the ground when they were got out of their stables and trotted up for us. We saw dodgy looking knees and legs with lumps and bumps on them. 'Sure, he got a little knock on the boat coming over, that's all,' seemed to be a popular excuse for deformities given by their Irish handlers. We were not going to bid for horses we were not completely happy about.

Then, just as we were resigned to the fact that we were going to be unlucky on the day, we saw a really impressive looking horse standing in a stable that we had ignored before. However, on checking his form it looked okay for our requirements. He had been placed in a couple of novice hurdles in Ireland for Henry de Bromhead (Gold Cup winning trainer) no less, and looked to be more the chasing type.

The reason he had not made our original shortlist was the fact he was sold 'as he stands' and not with a vet's certificate. Buying a horse without a vet's certificate was a red line we had not intended to cross. But, nevertheless, we asked him to be trotted up and, I must admit, he did move exceedingly well with a lovely long raking walk. A good race horse should always have a good walk. If he can walk well he can gallop well. He was excellently bred (by Yeats) and was a big dark bay, five years old. We all liked him, John included, and he was going through the ring not long after lunch.

We asked the selling trainer how much he would expect him to make and he told us there was, in fact, no reserve on him because he had to be sold come what may to settle a bad debt. He couldn't go back on the boat to Ireland.

We decided amongst ourselves that he was worth going up to £10,000 for, but not a penny more. At that price we thought he would be worth a try and something of a bargain considering, we discovered, he had gone through the ring for £23,000 only a month or two before.

After what seemed an agonisingly long time as the auctioneer kept going round and round the ring looking for a further bid, the hammer eventually fell at £10,000 exactly and he was the property of the Fellowship of the Rose Partnership. Black Market was his name – Mac to his friends.

So the dream continued. We had another horse. One this time definitely to go chasing. More reason for hope. More reason for expectation. It was also so exciting to finally see that hammer drop after so many 'last' rounds of the ring and then to know he was ours.

And there my story ends. Or, at least, for the purposes of this book it does, because, almost inevitably of course, there is going to be a whole story of its own about Mac, which would fill another volume.

So You Want to Own a Racehorse?

If you are now sufficiently inspired, after reading the story so far, to start a racing syndicate or partnership or maybe just join one to test the water, I have assembled a few ideas, tips, suggestions to help you on your way. They are, I would say, the basic requirements and important to consider.

1. Assuming you are on a budget and, in any case, we all want to get the best value for money, I would always settle upon a trainer who can give you an all-inclusive package. This would fix a monthly price for training. It means you pay exactly the same sum each month of the year whether your horse is in full training or having a month or two off in a field. The strong advantage is that you know what amount is going to come out of your account each month and can budget accordingly.

   To get transport costs included too is another big advantage as these can, otherwise, unexpectedly mount up and even put you off running a horse at a more far-flung course. If a trainer wants your business, they will normally agree to this option, probably subject to them transporting the horse within a certain radius of their stables.

2. Leasing could be a good, cheap, initial option. It means that there is no capital outlay to acquire a horse. If a trainer has a horse in the yard that they can offer on a lease it means that the ownership of the horse is transferred into your syndicate's name and runs in your colours for an agreed period of time. It is cheap (there is only a small admin cost) and easy to do and you have an 'instant' horse.

3. I would suggest drawing up a shortlist of four or five trainers and arrange to have a look around their stables and meet them to see how well you think you might get on with them. Feeling at ease with the trainer and just liking them as a person is so important. You may, of course, as I did with Peter, decide upon a certain trainer for whatever reason and not bother shopping around.

4. A trainer just setting out on their career may be a good option to consider. They may be more open to doing various training deals and may be happy to retain a certain percentage of the horse for themselves. They will certainly be keen to build up their numbers. The downside of course, is that they will, quite literally, have less of a track record.

5. Personally, I would always look for a trainer who, young or very experienced, has no more than about twenty-five horses in training at any one time. I think both you and your horse will stand a better chance of receiving personalised treatment and not be just a number. Communication between you and the trainer should be easier and you stand a better chance of feeling part of the set up.

6. It goes without saying that you will have to do all your sums very carefully before you start, but my advice is to give yourself

plenty of slack. For example, if you think that say, £150 per person per month should cover the costs, charge £175. Or, if you think the setup admin costs will be about £500, allow £800. All sorts of things can happen. People can pull out at the last minute, unexpected costs can arise. So always have some cash in reserve and you will sleep easier in your bed.

7. This next item may not be a problem at all if you are a small group of like-minded folk getting together to form a syndicate to follow your mutual passion for the sport. However, if you are starting a syndicate yourself and advertising for possible members, always state whether it is jumps or flat and stick to one or the other. Too many options only confuse people.

8. I will just mention one small warning. There are people around (too many) who will say to you in a fit of enthusiasm that they really want a share in your horse, but then, inexplicably, have changed their minds or just plain gone to ground when you start asking them for their money. Usually, I think it's either because they haven't got sufficient spare cash or that they got absolute hell when they mentioned it to their wife/husband/partner.

9. There are some costs which can catch you out if you haven't done enough research. You will have to budget for the cost of registering the name of your syndicate, registering your colours, registering your trainer with authority to act on your behalf (i.e., entering for races), registering for VAT statements. These will all mount up and don't forget the making up of the colours, which will be around the £180 mark depending on how complex they are. You may also find

it advantageous to register with the ROA (Racehorse Owners Association) VAT solutions scheme. It costs £135 per quarter and, basically, they reclaim all your VAT for you. Contact the ROA for details but it makes life simpler for you now that tax has gone digital, although it's not exactly cheap.

10. Talking of VAT, it is absolutely essential that you line up a sponsor before you form a syndicate. Once you have one you can register the syndicate for VAT which you can do via the HMRC website. The sponsorship thing is strange. The BHA did a deal a few years ago with the HMRC whereby if a horse is sponsored by a commercial company, the owners can claim all the VAT back on, for instance, training fees, jockey fees, etc. Now, some of the larger or better-known yards do have a yard sponsor. At Peter's it was Spillers. That makes things easy as your horse is just added to the yard sponsors list. If there is no yard sponsor though, there are two possible routes. One, contact the ROA and they will be able to arrange sponsorship by the Tote. Two, chat up a local business or maybe someone you know who runs a business (it can be very small) and ask them to become a sponsor. They are usually quite flattered and may even want to design their own sponsorship logo for the front of the silks. It only costs them £300 a year and they do get their name in the race card. You can always tell them that if your jockey gets interviewed their company name and logo will be seen by thousands on the telly. You could also offer them free or reduced-price owner's badges in return every time the horse runs and that gets them more involved that way. However you do it, it will save the syndicate thousands of pounds a year. In fact, it would be, in my opinion, very hard to run a syndicate, financially, without a sponsor and being VAT registered.

11. Deciding your racing colours can become a minefield if you let the prospective members of your syndicate have a say. Don't be democratic. For example, many will want, say, the colours of the football team they support and you could end up with one person wanting red and white, another blue and white, another claret and blue along with all the other suggestions for other personal reasons. The easiest way to sort things is to be autocratic and decide yourself what the silks will be. You can then reserve them, for free, on the BHA website. If you just announce to people that our colours are, for instance 'royal blue with white cross belts, red sleeves and red and blue quartered cap' everyone just accepts it and there can be no falling out.

12. You may be lucky enough to already know a trainer well enough to have no formal written agreement with them. Otherwise, get the agreement written down in black and white. Trainers are now in fact required to provide one so it is really just standard practice and they will probably have a template of one which they always use.

13. A written contract or agreement with the other owners is now compulsory. The BHA can check up that this is in place. Again, there is no big problem. When you start up your syndicate I would recommend following, once more, the BHA template. If you think you want or need to add any extra clauses, just do so, but the BHA guidance is very good. Let every member of the syndicate have a copy of the agreement to sign. No one will ever refuse to sign it because it is not onerous in any way.

14. If you do decide to advertise publicly for members, however, the rules change. Check on the BHA website again, but

publicly advertised shares in a horse are subject to much stricter rules and the agreement you have to produce reflects this. It is, basically, to protect members of the public from unscrupulous people who want to make a quick buck at their expense. I am sure you would not fall into that category and if the syndicate is to be formed of friends and family without advertising then you can ignore this piece of advice. But beware – just one advert anywhere and you will fall foul of this requirement. By the way, I have never had much luck advertising for members via the Racing Post, say or any other publication for that matter. It seems to attract the wrong sort of people attracted for the wrong reasons, like thinking they can get inside stable information for betting purposes. Steer clear of such folk.

15. So many people think, mistakenly, that you actually can make money out of owning a racehorse. Always point out that the chances of doing so, even on a modest scale, are so remote that you should abandon all hopes of doing so straight away. To break even, a horse would probably have to win at least three average sort of races a season and the number of horses who manage that, certainly consistently, is minuscule.

So explain to your syndicate that joining one is akin to taking out a golf club membership or gym membership except with that ever-so-slight chance that, via prize money and betting, you just might get some of your money back at the very best.

16. The trainer you go to may well have a horse in the yard ready to sell to you. If you like the look of the horse, it may be an idea to get it vetted before you buy and then, if you do buy it, have it looked over by a really good, recommended chiropractor or physiotherapist before it runs. Racehorses usually come with muscular-skeletal problems if they have previously raced and

these can be rectified to a large degree in the right hands. Making sure you find the right person to do the job can be a challenge but if you do the research and ask around there are some excellent specialist equine chiros and physios.

17. If you go to the sales always go with your trainer. They will know all the ropes and can bid for you if you want. From the sales catalogue, make a long list of possible purchases, then try and cut it down to a shorter list prioritising your requirements. Set a budget – this will preclude you even looking at quite a lot of horses. If you have any doubts about a horse, don't buy it. Don't be tempted into buying something just for the sake of it. If there is nothing in the sale – go to the next sale. There are plenty at Doncaster and there are other venues too. Always ask your trainer to search out any information they can about a particular horse you may be interested in. They usually know other trainers and have trusted contacts in other yards that can furnish them with potentially valuable information.

18. Just a warning about going to the sales. If you were to go with a budget of, say, £10,000, don't forget there is the VAT of 20 per cent on top of the sale price to pay and also the 6 per cent auctioneer's fee. The VAT you will be able to claim back if you register for VAT, which is absolutely essential, but you will still have to find the money up front. As soon as the hammer falls you will have to sign for that amount, although you later receive an invoice and have several weeks to settle it. You will also need a horsebox to take the horse immediately and somewhere for it to go. In reality, your trainer will arrange all that for you, but be careful!

19. After purchase, there will be all sorts of paperwork to do. You do not have to, but I would strongly advise you to set up a

bank account with Weatherby's bank. They are the bank that specifically services the racing industry. They are extremely helpful and easy to contact on the phone. A real person will always, instantly, pick up the phone and talk to you! Yes, really! All transactions concerning your horse and syndicate will go through the Weatherby's account. It means that entry fees, jockey fees and prize money will automatically be paid into and go out of your account without you having to worry about it. If only all banks were so accessible, friendly and efficient as Weatherby's! And no, I do not have shares in them – they are just plain good.

20. Well, now you have got your racehorse and soon it will be ready to run and expectations within your group will be running high. However, take time to explain to everyone, especially the ones who are new to racing and may not know too much about horses, that the trainer will probably want to give your purchase a few weeks to settle into his/her new surroundings. They will also want to have time to assess the horse's fitness. So it could be a few months even before it hits the track and you can all go racing. In other words – be patient. With horses patience is always a virtue, as I guess you will have gathered by now.

21. With that in mind never become downhearted because of lack of instant success. It is very, very difficult to get a winner. Think about it – if there is an average field size of ten runners there is always only one winner so you start off with a one in ten chance of being that winner. There are plenty of owners who have gone years before having their first winner having spent considerable sums of money whilst doing so. So be thankful if your horse comes back sound and well and able to fight another day. If the horse has

run as well as it possibly could on the day then be happy. And always remember that the handicapping system gives all horses a chance.

22. I have already mentioned getting your horse checked by a chiropractor but there will be times, almost inevitably, when your trainer will have to get the vet in (another potential cost, remember), but also don't close your mind to alternative treatments if necessary. For instance there is homeopathy, the use of magnets, water treadmills and all sorts of other possibilities that you should retain an open mind to. I personally can vouch for the efficacy of certain homeopathic treatments, so don't let people, particularly those in the medical and veterinary professions, convince you that it is mumbo jumbo or old wives' tales.

23. I would always try and see your horse as much as is possible for you and the syndicate members. It helps to get to know the horse as a 'person' rather than just see it as a name on a race card. If you are running a syndicate a get-together at fairly regular intervals at the stables is a good and popular idea, although I realise it depends to some extent on where the horse is stabled and where the owners live.

24. If you have a major problem with your trainer or feel that things are just not going as you would have hoped don't be afraid to consider changing trainers. All sorts of disputes can arise, large and small, but they should not persistently happen. Lack of truthful communication from the trainer is a not unheard of complaint, for instance, so, if you are unhappy with the yard over a period of time do start looking to move because it should not be like that. Conversely if you get on really well with the trainer in every way but have had,

so far, no success on the track I would advise against kicking him or her into touch too quickly. Relationships are very valuable and remember you went into ownership to get to the races as an owner and have fun. If you feel your trainer has become almost a friend and there is a mutual respect between you, then stick together and when that win comes it will be all the sweeter. Remember, if you want success at all cost you would first have to have mega bucks at your disposal to purchase a mega bucks horse, and I do not think that that is what we are all about at this level. Anyway I am sure that JP McManus has not had as much fun from racing as I have.

25. When you do eventually win a race or even get placed, don't forget to reward the stable staff if you can. It is always a good idea to slip the girl or lad looking after the horse on the day a tenner say. It keeps the staff on your side and it will be greatly appreciated by them and remembered. They all work very hard, don't get paid that much and they are the ones attending to your horse on a daily basis.

26. Spread the word. If you run a syndicate or are a member of one that could do with another few members to spread the cost drop out your experiences to people wherever you can without pushing it too much. You never know who might be interested in a share. If you dangle enough bait someone will eventually bite.

27. Always share your enthusiasm for the sport with as many people as you can, even those you don't think will be interested or might even be 'anti'. The 'antis' will say that racing, particularly jump racing, is cruel and that a lot of horses get killed whilst doing it and so on. Defend the cause

and fight your corner. We have nothing at all to be ashamed of. Quite the contrary. Point out that the most beautiful and amazing breed of horse – the thoroughbred – would not exist at all but for people wanting to race them. It is literally what they are bred to do. They love galloping and jumping. It is what they want to do in life and, as much as we can tell in an animal, they enjoy it. Do people really want to see the extinction of the thoroughbred? There are fatalities on the track, yes, but although there may be a few high profile ones in big races, the overall fatality rate is tiny, set against the number of runners, and is falling thanks to safety measures introduced over the past several years. It is a sport that will never be without its risks, but deaths and injuries leading to a horse's destruction are rare in the overall context. You can always point out that more horses (of all breeds) meet with fatal accidents just turned out into their field rather than whilst competing in any discipline.

28. Do join the ROA. The annual fee is worth every penny if only for one very good reason. It includes insurance cover for third-party liability. In other words, if your horse injures another horse or a person at a racecourse you have the peace of mind that you will not be risking possible personal bankruptcy because of a claim against you. That scenario has been known to happen to unfortunate owners before now. There are other benefits as well, of course. Your ROA membership card gets you free admission to most race meetings in the calendar even when you don't have a runner. Only the big meetings like Cheltenham or Royal Ascot are excluded. You may also want to take advantage of their VAT solutions service as already mentioned. Since tax has gone digital it makes it very costly for a small owner to invest in the required software and the ROA offer their

services to make the VAT claim on your behalf. The quarterly fee is not cheap but also not unreasonable and the service and communication from their small team (two people I think) is excellent.

Horse Racing

And finally – it occurred to me that any reader of this, despite their obvious interest in racing, may still be baffled or confused by certain common pieces of racing terminology and jargon surrounding the process of actually deciding where to enter your horse and then getting him/her to the right race at the right location. I am sure I have already used several of these terms myself in this book so, in order for you to hold your own with any of the professional racing fraternity you may be about to encounter, here are a few explanations that I hope may be helpful if not entirely exhaustive.

Types of Races

For a start we know, of course, that that there are two types of racing, which is a slightly different notion to the one above. There is jump (otherwise National Hunt) racing and there is flat racing. As you will have gathered I have little or no interest in the latter, but I'll do my best to outline the types of races available under both codes.

Flat racing is just flat racing. Cynics might say that they just canter down to the start and then gallop back again. Job done.

National Hunt racing, however, is divided into three types. There are National Hunt flat races, hurdle races and steeplechases. The National Hunt flat races, or bumpers as they are very often referred to, are purely meant as an introduction to the racecourse for young future jumps horses. They are run usually over two miles, occasionally maybe one mile six furlongs, and are restricted to horses who have never run on the flat and are aged seven years or under. In Great Britain you can only run a horse in bumpers three times and then they must go over jumps. In Ireland the rules on that may differ. It's a good idea as it enables a young horse to learn to gallop around a racecourse without the added complication of jumping hurdles, but it is a system that has been known to have been abused where flat-bred horses whose future is on the flat have been entered in bumpers in order to pick up easy prize money. A decent flat-bred horse will always be that bit quicker than most jump bred horses, if they are able to stay the two miles distance that is.

Hurdle races are run over a minimum of two miles and the hurdles are the lower obstacles, the sort that can be knocked down, although you always want your horse to jump them! The best hurdlers tend to skim over the hurdles and the pace in hurdle races is consequently faster than equivalent chases. There are a few courses, Southwell, Haydock and Worcester to my knowledge, that have brush hurdles, which can't be knocked down and are almost like mini steeplechase fences. As the name suggests they are made of brush.

Steeplechases are run over the higher birch fences, the tops of which can just about be brushed through at most courses but, again, the object of the exercise is for the horse to clear the obstacles. It usually requires a taller, larger framed horse to be a good steeplechaser but there are always exceptions. Look at Tiger Roll for instance, a diminutive horse who didn't have an exactly bad Grand National record.

As for the actual types of races you will see listed on a typical day's race card, some are common to both codes whilst others relate to either one code or the other.

Common to both flat and jumps are:
   Maidens – races that are restricted to those horses that have never won a race under that code.
   Novices – races open to maidens but also to horses who have not won a race before the end of the previous season, although previous winners usually have to carry extra weight (a penalty).
   Sellers – races where the winner is offered to public auction after the race. All the other horses in the race can also be claimed.
   Claimers – races where each of the participants can be bought after the race for a pre-registered price decided by the owner or trainer. The higher the price required the higher the weight the horse will run off.
   Handicaps – races where horses are allotted a weight according to their handicap rating so that horses of varied ability can race competitively against each other.

Types of races for the flat only are:
   Stakes – races where the horses carry equal weights but usually within a given banding of handicap ratings. For example for horses rated say 0–70.
   Auction Races – races designed for horses who have been purchased for a price at the lower end of the spectrum, therefore for horses of supposedly of lesser ability (but not necessarily).

Types of races for the jumps only are:
   Hunter Chases – races restricted to amateur riders and horses that have a certificate to show they have taken part in hunting that season.
   Beginners Chase – races for horses that are maidens over steeplechase fences.
   Graduation Chases – races for horses that have not won more than two steeplechases.

Juvenile Hurdles – races restricted to three-year-olds before 1 January and to four-year-olds from 1 January until the end of the season.

There may be some other arcane classifications tucked away somewhere in the rules of a racing hand book but I think the above list will cover any race that you trainer might suggest for your horse. The next thing to mention is how races are classed according to their importance and their prize money. The two usually go hand in hand anyway.

Classes of Races

The first way of classifying races is ever so simple. That in itself is a rarity for horse racing, which always seems to like to complicate matters. Straightforwardly put a class 1 race is the highest class and a class 7 race is the lowest. Yes, it's as easy as that. Well not quite, because the scale in jump racing only goes down to class 6. The class 6 races in National Hunt is for bumpers and hunter chases, otherwise they follow the same pattern with class 1 races being for the highest-rated horses, down to class 5 for the lowest rated ones. In jump races all novice non-handicap races are class 4.

You may also encounter the terms graded races 1 to 3, group races, listed races, pattern races and black type. To have any personal involvement in any of these races you would have to have an excessively talented horse, but you just never know your luck. They all relate to the very best and most valuable and prestigious races. The group races represent the very pinnacle of horse racing on the flat whilst over the jumps the Cheltenham Gold Cup for instance is one of a relatively few grade 1 races – the pinnacle for National Hunt. Without getting bogged down in infinite detail the other classifications are at the absolute top end of the spectrum too and the 'black type' refers to the dark typeface used in sales catalogues to indicate past winners of top-class races in a horse's pedigree. This is very important to breeders and to potential buyers when assessing an unraced young horse's possible ability.

The Handicapping System

The handicapping system is something that has already, inevitably cropped up quite a bit in this book. It is hardly surprising since most races are handicaps and it is a system at the very heart of horse racing. As I have already said somewhere it is the object of the handicapper to get all the runners in a race to cross the line together in a kind of giant dead heat. The handicapper never succeeds in doing quite that but it is a mechanism to try and give all the horses in a given race an equal chance of winning and it has been tried and tested over many years.

When I say 'the handicapper' there are, in fact, a number of persons (all male still I believe) employed by the BHA to do the job. They tend to be given responsibility for different types or races. Some will deal with flat others with jumps. Some will deal with two-mile hurdlers and others with three-mile chasers and so on. All of them, though, really do study the form of each individual horse, however lowly that horse may be, and try to assess its current ability based on its latest runs. Some people criticise handicappers for being swift to put up a horse's handicap mark when it wins whilst being very slow to bring it down again if it starts to lose. But I honestly believe they do a painstaking and fair assessment of each horse and, if occasionally they do get things slightly wrong, a trainer can always phone them up make a plea for their horse to be treated more leniently because of this, that or the other factor. As long as the trainer is civil to them the handicapper will always take a second look and see if they have a point. If I were a trainer I would certainly never want to fall out with one. I do know you want to keep them on your side.

The theory of handicapping is based on the fact that one pound of extra weight a horse carries slows him down by one length. Therefore, if one horse would normally beat another by ten lengths on equal weights, if it were to carry ten extra pounds the two horses would finish equal. Weight really does slow horses down, although, always remember, lack of weight can't make a very slow horse go any faster!

Under the saddle there is a saddle cloth known as a weight cloth and in this weight cloth small lead weights can be inserted. The jockeys have to sit on the scales before the start of each race carrying the saddle to make sure the correct weight will be carried in the race. After the race they repeat the process to make sure all the lead weights are still where they should be!

The handicap mark that a horse is given by the handicapper reflects its assessed ability and is expressed in lbs. A horse rated 100, for instance, is 5lbs or five lengths inferior in ability to a horse rated 105. The handicapper has to wait until a horse has three completed starts to its name before a mark can be given and up to that point the horse would have to run in level weight novice races.

The scale of ratings, it is important to point out, is different between the two codes with horses in jump racing having the higher ratings. A Cheltenham Gold Cup winner would have a rating in excess of 170 whilst a Derby winner would be rated, say, in excess of 130.

Under both codes though, horses of a similar ability will race against each other off different weights but within bands of ability; 0–100 is the lowest rating band in jump racing and 0–45 is the lowest on the flat.

The Going

The going can certainly be all important to some horses and can determine how they are going to perform for you. Remember Fiddlers Flight joyously sloshing through the mud whilst others struggled. Be patient with your trainer if they are waiting for the correct ground. It can make all the difference and can be worth waiting for and will avoid disappointment with your horse.

The going classifications as given by the clerk of the course before the start of each meeting are straightforward and are as follows:

Hard – Firm – Good to Firm – Good – Good to Soft – Soft – Heavy

You can see there is a logical symmetry to this with 'good' being the mid-point. However, it is worth pointing out that, although jump racing can frequently take place during the depths of the British winter on heavy ground, it will never take place these days on hard ground. Some horses may not like the heavy going but their legs will be safe on it. However, any horse galloping and jumping on hard ground is likely to come back with an injured leg of some sort which could end its career. Even firm ground nowadays is considered by most to be unraceable for jumps horses and so you will find that all courses staging summer National Hunt meetings will water the ground to try and maintain good to firm going at the very least. In my humble opinion I would not even consider running a horse over obstacles unless the ground was being given at least as good, preferably good to soft, even if I did have a horse that relished the faster ground. I would want my horse to come back with its legs intact.

I should mention that in going reports in Ireland you may come across the term 'yielding', which is equivalent to our 'good to soft'.

You will also, no doubt, come across the going stick figures which are mentioned in most going reports now. Basically, the clerk of the course has a stick with a device on the end of it which, when it is inserted into the ground, will tell you the firmness or softness of the turf. The higher the reading that it gives, the firmer the ground. So eight is getting plenty hard enough whilst four is very sloppy. These readings are a useful indication as to the state of the going but they are only an indication. The clerk of the course still has to make a judgement themself as to what official going they are going to give. In other words, going reports are still as much an art as a science. It is also not uncommon for the going to be altered during the course of the meeting. If it suddenly starts to rain heavily that is understandable but sometimes it is changed in response from the reports coming in from the jockeys as they return from the race. Jockeys have a good feel for the going that they are racing on and it is always worth listening to what their assessment is.

Entries and Declarations

Entering your horse for a race and then declaring to run is ultimately what it is all about. Of course your trainer as your appointed agent will, in reality, handle this for you, but this is how the system works. Horses, except for a handful of top races, have to be entered by twelve noon six days before the scheduled race. As I say, a few races have to be entered several weeks in advance but these are races at the Cheltenham Festival for example, or the Grand National or the Derby. So back to reality. If your race is on a Tuesday entries will close the previous Wednesday. They are called, you will notice in the racing press, five-day entries but, in reality, they are made six days prior to the race. Don't ask. As a rule of thumb, and this is far from an exact science, the number of horses that actually end up running in the race is around half of those that are entered. So do not panic if you see there are twenty-eight entries for a race that can only have sixteen runners (for safety reasons). It's a reasonable bet that all those who want to run will end up getting into the race in the instance above. There are lots of reasons why a horse doesn't end up being declared. It may pick up an injury, the ground may go against it, it may do a very poor piece of work at home, it may be entered for other similar races elsewhere. There are all sorts of reasons.

Some races with lots of entries will see some horses, however, not getting in the race. If it is a handicap the horses with the lowest handicap marks will be the first out. If it is not a handicap but, say, a novice race on equal weights, there is a ballot and the horse drawing the lowest number will be the first to be balloted out, although previous winners or previously placed horses are given preference to run. There are the usual arcane rules surrounding all this but that is the nub of it. By the way, if your race is on a Saturday your entry day would be the Monday because you cannot make an entry on a Sunday (although you can declare on the Sabbath).

If you and your trainer decide your horse is going to run then they have to declare it as a runner before 10 a.m. two days before the race. A horse can be declared and withdrawn if it has to be but not after 9:30 a.m.. It can sometimes be nerve wracking to see if you are going to get in the race or not but it is always interesting to see who and how many you are going to be up against. And so there you are. About ninety minutes later you can go on the Racing Post or Sporting Life websites and see your horse's name on the race card with your colours and not just the jockey's but the owner's name as well for all to behold. The first time you see that it's a tremendous thrill and at that point the anticipation of the race can begin in earnest. During the afternoon the BHA will email you (if you are the actual owner or running the syndicate) inviting you to reserve your owner's badges for yourself and friends and you can look forward to your first day of, it is to be hoped, many days at the races as an owner.

An Afterthought

Just as an afterthought. I was at a race meeting very recently where our current horse (Black Market) was due to be running but had to be taken out of his race because the going had changed and was now too firm, when I bumped into a chap I had not seen for very nearly fourteen years. We looked at each other briefly, as you do when you are not quite sure if you're really recognising the other person. Then he came up to me and said, 'Phil! Nice to see you. It's been an awfully long time.' I explained why I was there and assumed at first that he was just having a day at the races, remembering that he lived close to that course. But he said, 'No. In fact I shall have to dive off soon because we have a runner in the next race. I started my own syndicate after I left you, you know, and now, believe it or not, we've got four horses running for us. I tested the water with the Fellowship of the Rose and it was you who inspired me to have a go at it myself and it's been great. So thank you very much. Mind you, if I'd known it was such bloody hard work I don't know if I'd have bothered!'

We laughed at that, shook hands and he made his way off to look after his own little 'flock' as they made their way excitedly into the parade ring. It was quite a warm and satisfying feeling to know that because I had formed my own humble, low-budget syndicate all that time ago, I had so positively affected somebody

An Afterthought

else's life all these years later – not to mention the lives of all his syndicate members.

So if you still think you want to own a racehorse, what's stopping you? Go for it – and good luck.